Adapt to Adopt

A Human Approach to Software Implementation

Dr. Anna Hunter, EdD

Adapt to Adopt

A Human Approach to Software Implementation

Editor: Brett Peruzzi / PeruzziCommunications.com

BookDesign / Art Direction: Rob Levine/ levinedesign.net

Library of Congress Control Number: 2023916758

ISBN: 9781941573891

Published by Damianos Publishing
2 Central Street, Studio #152
Framingham, MA 01701 USA
DamianosPublishing.com

Produced through Silver Street Media by Bridgeport National Bindery, Agawam, MA USA

First printed 2023

This book was printed on paper from sources committed to rigorous forest management standards, developing, and promoting sources of renewable energy, using recycled fiber and materials, and promoting forest certification in the U.S. and around the world. SFI (Sustainable Forestry Initiative), and FSC (Forest Stewardship Council).

(FSC Certification ensures that products come from responsibly managed forests that provide environmental, social and economic benefits to those forestry areas. The FSC Recycled label indicates that the product was made from 100% recycled materials.)

SUSTAINABLE FORESTRY INITIATIVE
SFI-00001

FSC
100%
From well-managed forests
FSC® C000000

To my readers.

May you find the courage
to put your people first.

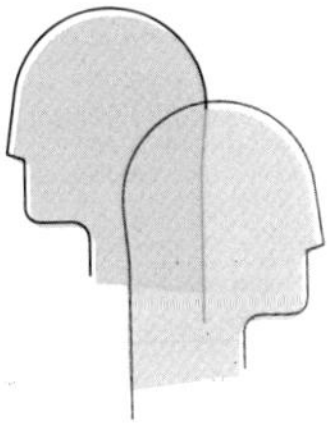

Table of Contents

What You Can Expect from This Book

I have read countless books on software implementation and business improvement. While many of them include information about users and teams, the people-side of software adoption is usually limited to a few chapters. This is fascinating because the people behind the scenes are critical to its value in an organization. I have yet to find a book that is dedicated to the experience of people who need to adopt and use new software. Well, that changes today.

This book is centered on the people in your organization who are impacted by the changes that accompany software implementation. My unique background in counseling, adult learning, organizational development, change management, and of course, software implementation positions me well to delve into this often overlooked topic. I encourage you to pause and take a step back from your daily grind to truly consider the human side of implementation. Don't get me wrong, I am a huge advocate for software that will benefit an organization and help your team achieve its mission. I simply argue that creating a strategy which is focused on navigating change with your people is just as important (if not more important) as the software implementation itself. Imagine having your dream car with no fuel. You have the necessary equipment, but are missing the critical resource to make it run. The same concept can be applied to having a robust new software system with no people bought in to operate it. Your people are the fuel that will keep the software engine running. So this is your chance to tap into the human side of implementing software. After all, they will determine if it is a success.

As long as I can remember, I've always been enthusiastic about new ideas, concepts, and innovations. While I met many new ideas with initial skepticism, as soon as I latched onto one, I would push forward full throttle and try to convince everyone around me to buy in. I thought my excitement and enthusiasm alone would be enough to convince people to hop on the bandwagon. It wasn't until I was fed a huge dose of reality during my counseling program that I realized everyone around me responds to change differently. My underlying goal in getting others to join in was less about helping them and more about gaining affirmation for the new idea.

During our counseling rotations, my professors watched while I gave what I thought was invaluable advice to a client. I was so excited that I "cracked the code," and believed I knew the perfect steps for my client to make long-term changes in their life. To my surprise, the professors ended my counseling session early and sat me down to rewatch a recording of the session. After the recording ended, their one question to me was, "Who was the session about?" I knew the answer they would want to hear and quickly responded by saying "my client." Then they put me on the spot and asked me to explain how the session focused on my client. It became clear that while I had the best intentions, I focused on the value I thought I could provide to the client rather than focusing on the client themself. This moment was pivotal, because I learned that I will never fully understand someone else's experience enough to give them advice. The best I can do is empathize and try to provide enough support for them to fulfill their own needs. This book will provide tons of insight into how you can develop a strategy for putting your employees first when introducing new software. You may not understand or relate to their experiences directly, yet practicing the principles outlined in the following chapters will help you gain enough insight to support them as you navigate the change process together. Please remember that your employees will always know what is best for them. When in doubt, go to the source to discover their needs.

This book is designed as a hands-on experience which walks you through several exercises for navigating the software implementation process. To benefit the most from the material, download a free printable workbook from my website: www.anna-hunter.com/book.

Note:

We are on the cusp of a new era, having easy and quick access to artificial intelligence (AI) tools that could write an entire book for us in a few minutes. It is only fair of me to disclose the role of AI in this publication. After all, we are discussing software adoption. I have embraced the benefit that AI provides for increased efficiency in day-to-day tasks. Yet to provide a unique perspective derived from my personal background and experience, I have chosen not to leverage assistance from AI technology in the process of writing this book. The purpose of this book is to focus on the people behind software and I imagine our trust would be compromised if I let a computer do the talking.

I also admit that I am personally navigating the change process as I anticipate and discover ways that AI will alter my work and personal life. So the guidance I offer you in the subsequent chapters is relevant as you consider yourself as someone who is leading the charge and first-hand as you are personally impacted by the introduction of new software.

1 Why Change?

"The rate at which organizations learn may soon become the only sustainable source of competitive advantage."

– Ray Stata

The topic of change is near and dear to my heart as I was raised upon a foundation of uncertainty. Being one of seven children, I had to be ready for change at every given moment. I was either adjusting to inconsistent schedules, adapting to my siblings' needs, or joining my parents at a new job site week by week. An established, steady routine was a concept I never knew. Did I mention my dad was a general contractor? This meant that the typical nine a.m. to five p.m. workday was unheard of! I often found myself settling into a unique balance of uncertainty and comfort. As I look back, I realize that traces of my upbringing not only prepared me for the inevitable change that surrounds me each day, but my past also led to a passion for fostering change resilience in others.

I am an early millennial who lived through the evolution of eight-tracks to cassette tapes, CDs to iPods, and now the digital music library of today. Wall-mounted landline phones were revolutionized when cordless phones were introduced, but quickly replaced with car phones, cell phones, and just about every smart communication device you can imagine! We realized that all new technology is temporary and we're groomed to seek out the *next best thing*. The only guarantee that we can count on is change itself. So I ask myself, "Why aren't we taking the time to understand the emotional experience of change?"

Let's dive into the impact of change on people who are directly affected by new software and how you can make sure that your employees are adopting the change that you are trying to instill. When broaching this topic of conversation, I am often met with an all-or-nothing perspective that sounds a little something like: "We are going to change, so people need to get on board or get out of the way." The "deal with it" approach can impede a leader's ability to foster change that sticks. What we are aiming for is a transformational leader who recognizes that people are the greatest asset in an organization and the most successful change is achieved through having *all hands on deck*. Industries are driven by competition. Our greatest opportunity for having a competitive edge is through our people. They produce the results so we need to invest in them. It is not only in a leader's best interest to be in tune with employee experiences throughout the change process, but doing so will foster sustainable organizational growth.

Leaders reach organizational goals through a balance of concern for people and concern for results. A genuine concern for people is shown by attending to their needs and ensuring high engagement. On the other hand, concern for results focuses on production and the achievement of tasks. Striking a balance for both increases the chances of employee involvement, strengthening their commitment to change while bolstering the outcome of the change. Taking this one step further, as leaders, we must also manage our own emotions and involvement during the change process. Employees are counting on us to guide them toward the light at the end of the tunnel. So leading with calm energy, clarity, and confidence provides an anchor amid the mucky waters that underpin change.

The key to effectively leading toward organizational success is through seeking personal balance, employee balance, and balance in vision. Equilibrium is achieved through constant reflection, evaluation, and prioritization. You may feel as though you are "cracking a code" or trying to find the best recipe that will have the greatest impact. This feeling can be channeled and leveraged to serve as your motivation through the process.

Additionally, leaders should create a safe space for their employees to openly voice their concerns and opinions. Approach your employees with curiosity through observation and inquiry by withholding assumptions and adjusting to meet their specific needs. A safe space welcomes open debate, respectful dissent, and unbridled idea sharing. As you explore the practices outlined in this book, leverage individual and group check-ins, informal observation, and general inquiry with your team to gain insight into their experiences. When you notice an imbalance, simply make incremental adjustments until an equilibrium is restored.

The People Behind Software

Change is inevitable, and I'd even go so far as to say that change is one of the few certainties we have in life. The only way to ensure your business is sustainable is through change. The world is evolving and if we don't evolve with it, we're behind. A driving factor of this evolution is that consumer expectations are growing, which challenge organizations to rapidly change in response to external pressures. While the ability for an organization to respond and adapt to these pressures equips them with the tools necessary for long-term growth, the negative impact of frequent change on employees can be significant.

We can take time to examine the way countless instruments of change impact employees, yet the one that stands out most in this era is software implementation. The use of software in organizations has become a minimum standard, even more so with cloud-based Software as a Service (SaaS) adding value by increasing efficiencies and streamlining workflows. We often find ourselves shopping around for new solutions, although we may already have access to several that could meet our needs. New software is being developed every day that threatens competitors who have become accustomed to monopolizing specific markets and industries. According to BetterCloud, organizations use an average of 130 SaaS applications (BetterCloud, 2023). The use of multiple software programs becomes a sort of technology network or ecosystem, which can be overwhelming for those required to use them on a daily basis.

I'm sure we can all agree that the evolution of software exposes us to a never-ending library of new technology. For some, exploring new software is a thrilling adventure. For others, it is a daunting and overwhelming experience. Regardless of your employees' reception to new software, their role in establishing its value in your organization is undeniable. As much as we try (and we are making major strides in this direction), software does not completely run itself, nor does it stand alone as a solution. It is merely a component within a larger system that also encompasses the people involved and the data that is traveling through it. People are truly the power behind the machines; whether entering inputs or receiving outputs, they determine the value of the software within a system. Let's explore this in more detail.

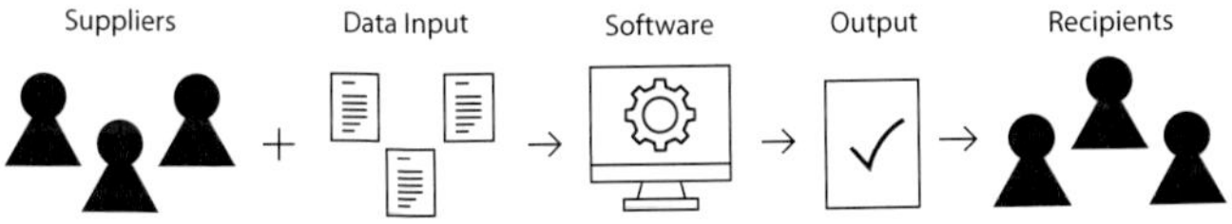

We start with the *who*; who are the suppliers of information? Our data input is the *what*; the information that is fed into the software. The software is the *how*; how are we creating value from the data that was input? The output is another *what*; what are we getting out of the process? Finally, the recipients are the other *who*; those who are benefiting from the valuable output. To summarize, people supply information or data inputs to the software, then the software creates more value out of this information and, in turn, provides valuable insights or outputs to the end users. Take invoicing software for example. The *suppliers* are employees who input the items and amounts to be invoiced into the software. The *software* adds value by transferring the data onto professionally formatted invoice documents, saving the data, providing reports, and maintaining records. Perhaps the software even allows online payment processing. The *output* of a professional invoice and an online payment processing option is then received by the *recipient* or customer who benefits from a clear and simple method for paying their invoice.

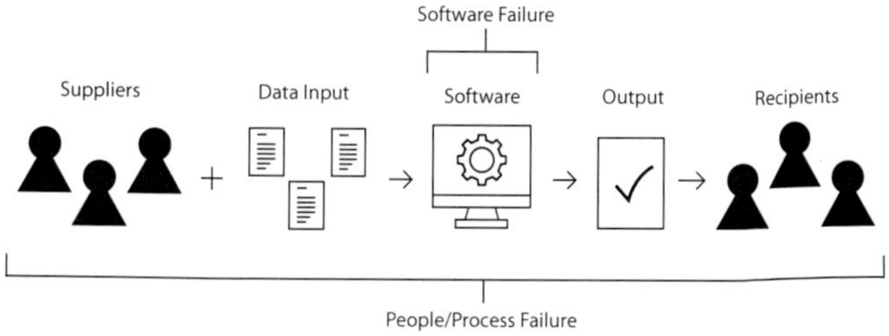

There are two kinds of failure we can face when software is a part of our system. When the software itself is not capable of adding the value that you need, it needs to be reconsidered. We often notice this when the output is falling short of your recipients' expectations. On the other hand, the most common failure arises when the data fed into the software is not sufficient enough to deliver a successful outcome. This is a people and process issue. Ultimately, the outcome will only be as good as the input. If your people are not contributing high value inputs, then the software will not provide successful value to the process. Employee buy-in of new technology has a direct influence on the quality of information provided, frequency of use, integration into business processes, and overall commitment to the change.

Successful change is initiated early and methodically. This means right now you should be thinking about the change you're going to make one year, three years, and even five years down the line. Too often we are thinking about the change we hope to make tomorrow or next week. While adapting quickly is the key to an agile organization, quick changes should take place sparingly until you build an agile team culture. To effectively anticipate future change, we must think about next year, then think about the next five years, and ask ourselves, "What trends are happening?"

Don't ignore new trends or technology, but rather be curious and dig in. Approach all evolution with curiosity and you'll be in a good position.

2 The Nature of Change

"Leading in a culture of change means creating a culture (not just a structure) of change. It does not mean adopting innovations, one after another; it does mean producing the capacity to seek, critically assess, and selectively incorporate new ideas and practices—all the time, inside the organization as well as outside it."

- Michael Fullen, *Leading in a Culture of Change* (2001)

You might argue that the outcome of change, in this case software implementation, is the most important part of the process. While we are indeed working toward an outcome that should contribute to organizational success, the most impactful phase of the change process is actually before the change is even underway. Adequate time spent preparing for the introduction of a new software system will be returned in dividends when you and your employees are seamlessly navigating the change. Now, if you are reading this book while the change process is already underway, don't worry. All this information is still relevant; in fact, you might find the need to backtrack in the process so you can make adjustments and ensure successful employee adoption.

Types of Change

Each organization experiences change differently. How change is navigated at an organization level can significantly impact employee adoption. The most common patterns of change are measured by the rate of change as experienced by organizations over time (Grundy 1993).

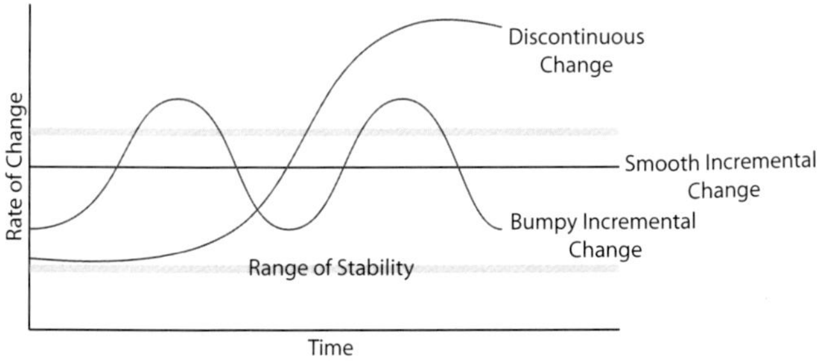

Adapted from Major Types of Change (Grundy 1993).

Smooth Incremental Change

Organizations that experience smooth incremental change have slow evolution of transition. All change contributes to a greater vision and follows a clear path. When it occurs, change is often minor and continuous. This gives employees enough stability and predictability to cope with the change process. While this type of change may seem ideal, it is less and less common given our rapid societal evolution.

Bumpy Incremental Change

This type of change occurs frequently, but without consistency. When change is experienced, it is more accelerated with lulls between the change processes. The predictability experienced here is the change itself as it tends to be a continuous process and is expected as part of the organizational culture. Yet sudden peaks of rapid change may push employees out of their comfort zones. This is often the case when responding to external factors such as new market trends or changes in the environment. This pattern of change is also common when organizations respond to internal factors like bringing on new software that can accommodate an increased staff size. Although it may feel unstable at times, employees can often tolerate this change.

Discontinuous Change

This type of change is characterized by a radical shift away from the existing, stable state. Often in response to an external crisis, an organization may need to make a fast, immediate change to adapt. Leaders in an organization may provide directives to their employees rather than take time to guide them through the change process. Examples of this could be introducing new compliance or security software in response to a data breach. This type of change should be used sparingly to avoid creating a culture of imbalance and instability.

Continuous Transformation

Today, we might see more frequent and continual change on a regular basis. Let's call this continuous transformation with the goal of reaching sustainable growth. Rapid advancements in technology have pushed frequent change among organizations. We find ourselves trying to keep up with growing expectations from customers, let alone staying on the cutting edge. This rapid transformation and growth will require an organization and its employees to be extremely agile and willing to embrace new advancements. The sooner you gain understanding of how to support and guide your employees through change, the more agile your organization will become. The goal is to ensure your employees feel confident through the change process so they embrace all your future endeavors.

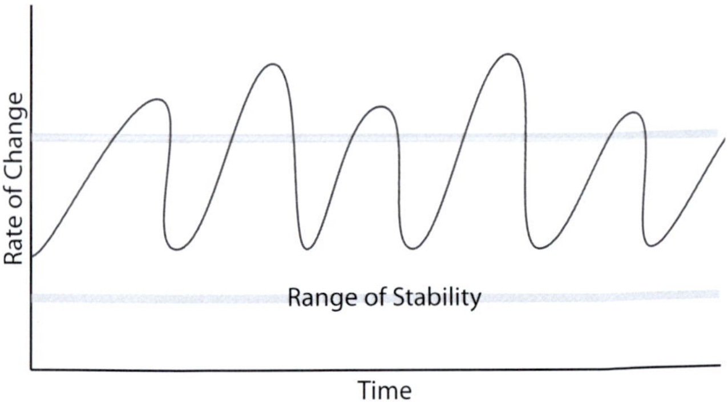

Reflect on the change that has taken place within your own organization. How would you describe the type of change that has occurred so far? Do you find that you are changing in response to internal needs or external pressures? How much control do you feel you have over your organization's change? How are your employees responding to the frequency of change in your organization?

Change-Based Culture

An organization is more than the sum of its individuals. The interaction between people is powerful. Put simply, if we used a mathematical equation to measure the value of people in our organization, addition just wouldn't cut it. Multiplication would be much more suitable. As organizations evolve, several organic components contribute to its culture, which are often informal in nature. One of the most significant influences on team culture are the norms established by the people within it. Norms are behaviors or traditions that are accepted and agreed upon, or simply understood, within a team. They provide a sense of "normalcy" or comfort and consistency that team members count on. When change disrupts organizational norms, people can begin to feel uneasy and unstable. So the degree to which employees are committed to group norms gives insight into their capacity for and level of resistance to change.

Imagine that you were standing in front of the room during a team meeting and the lights were turned down low. Suddenly a spotlight was focused on you and this was the time you planned to introduce new software to your team. After your announcement, your employees all pushed back their seats and gave you a standing ovation with huge smiles on their faces as if you just solved all their problems. Wouldn't that be nice? Although we can't guarantee that kind of a reaction, as you continue to build an agile culture, this vision could be your goal. Aim to foster a culture in your organization that is adaptive to, and even excited by change. My typical mantra as a leader is to "expect the unexpected." In fact it is a motto that my employees live by each and every day. Occasionally I ask them, "What is one unexpected thing that will happen today?" The answer should be "I don't know" and we need to learn to be comfortable with that. As we're thinking about fostering a culture of change in our organization, agility is key.

This will be more difficult for some than others, and we will explore the reasons behind this challenge. As soon as your employees understand and are prepared for your organization being in a constant state of change, you will be unstoppable. As leaders, it's important to teach that we cannot grow if we remain in our comfort zone. Therefore, we must step out of our comfort zone and be uncomfortable in order to experience growth. Think about how you can foster a change-based culture that supports productive discomfort, as long as we are growing as a result. Sometimes this means arriving at the office and asking your employees the most random question about themselves. They might be immediately caught off guard, but even in seemingly small ways, you are intentionally creating a culture that is adaptive.

Now is the time to ask ourselves, "How can we gradually bend and influence the culture without causing heightened disruption?" Once we can answer this question, we will be prepared to guide our employees toward a culture shift. I find that newer organizations tend to have a more agile culture than established organizations. There is usually less bureaucracy and red tape established in new organizations, not to mention that they were founded during a time of rapid evolution. As you can imagine, shaping a culture will most likely take longer for larger and more established organizations, while taking less time and effort for smaller, newer organizations. While determining the best way to influence a culture, a safe assumption is that the change process is most meaningful when leaders inspire self-discovery among their employees. I like to foster an environment that encourages curiosity, creativity, and active involvement in the change process, which guides my employees toward discovery and innovation. Think of this well-known proverb: "Give a man a fish and you feed him for a day; teach a man to fish and you feed him for a lifetime." When thinking long term, it is more worthwhile to teach or inspire someone to do something for themselves than to simply do it for them. This principle can also be applied to leading change. Refrain from "feeding" information and knowledge to others, but provide them with a path toward their own growth. By doing so, you can guide employees through a reflective change process while mitigating initial apprehension. This will also prepare them for navigating future change that is to come.

3 Adapting to Change

"Change has a considerable psychological impact on the human mind. To the fearful it is threatening because it means that things may get worse. To the hopeful it is encouraging because things may get better. To the confident it is inspiring because the challenge exists to make things better."

– King Whitney Jr.

What is change adoption as it relates to software implementation? Successful adoption is shown when users accept and embrace the new software as part of their standard workflows. Team adoption is the most essential ingredient in software implementation as it brings the solution to life and solidifies its worth in your organization. We are used to thinking about the big picture regarding how the new software will impact our organization as a whole and then proceed to announce the changes to our employees. Team adoption, in this case, becomes an afterthought. Instead, I'd like to remind you to think through how the new software will impact your employees' roles and responsibilities. Consider the change from each employee's perspective and then develop strategies to foster buy-in, so you are prepared to lead the charge while meeting their needs.

Social Influence

If you are reading this book, chances are, you are already anticipating some type of resistance for the new software you are hoping to implement. I hear a very common narrative when working with leaders who are introducing new software to their teams and it sounds a little something like this: "There are a few people on my team who just hate technology. They are like dinosaurs. They will never change." As we consider our past experiences with employees, it's easy to fall into the assumption that they will respond to this change in the same way. Let's break this down a bit further.

Change adoption is heavily affected by social influence. The Diffusion of Innovation theory was made popular by Everett Rogers in 1962. His theory outlines how, why, and the rate at which new ideas spread, specifically in the technology arena. Rogers explains five key elements that contribute toward the spread of a new idea: the idea itself, adopters, communication channels, time, and a social system. An idea must be widely adopted through social capital in order to be self-sustaining and ultimately reach critical mass. Rogers presents a model that shows the widespread response employees may have when presented with a new idea. You can probably recognize where some of your employees fall within this model as we walk through each section.

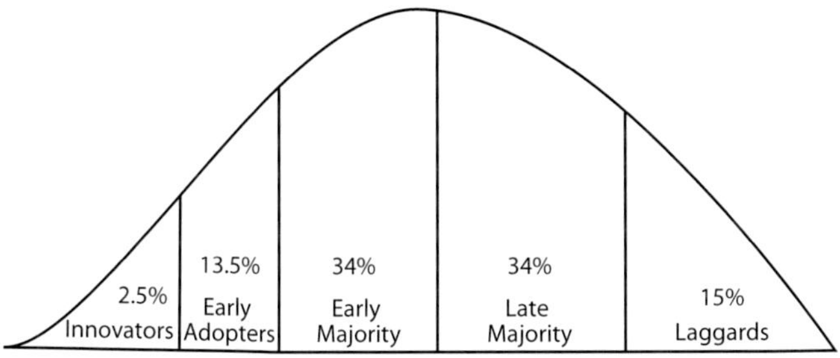

Adapted from Diffusion of Innovation Model (Rogers 1962).

A very small percentage of people within organizations are considered *Innovators*. They are often willing to take risks and they may even crave the change process. They cope well with uncertainty and take it upon themselves to ensure they are very well informed. I often refer to the Innovators as the movers and shakers in the organization. While they help us think outside the box and consider alternative solutions to solving problems, they may not consider how others navigate the change process differently than themselves.

The *Early Adopters* are probably the most pivotal group as they are the employees that will have the most influence over others in your organization. Some might consider them gatekeepers of all new ideas. Since they are opinion leaders, they can either make or break a successful change process. If they are on board with the change, they will move mountains in gaining buy-in from other employees. If they are not on board…well, let's just say that it will be worth your while to spend some extra time and energy to win them over! As the most influential group within your organization, you will benefit by keeping your eye on them.

It is quite common that we encounter employees who take some time to warm up to change. They often look to others in the organization to decide how to react when change is on the horizon. Welcome to the *Early Majority*! People who fall in this category don't often respond to new ideas with immediate resistance, but they withhold a concrete opinion until they hear from others whom they trust. Once approval and trust is gained through Early Adopters, the Early Majority is bound to follow.

Another healthy portion of your employees is made up of the *Late Majority*. They tend to meet change with skepticism and it usually takes some time for them to get on board with adopting a new idea. If you do win over someone from the Late Majority, it is often a result of peer pressure from others. Since the Late Majority is not easily swayed, introducing new ideas early and giving them more time to digest the change is beneficial.

Lastly are the *Laggards*, who tend to be more socially isolated from the rest of your employees. They can be the most suspicious about change and the people who are driving the change forward. They are also not easily influenced by Early Adopters. To accommodate this group, it is important that you start the process early and communicate the vision for the change at the beginning. This not only helps them understand the purpose of the change, but also gives them confidence and trust throughout the process. Context is key for Laggards, so when in doubt, provide the who, what, where, when, and why for each new idea and give them time to ask questions.

As you can imagine, the ways in which employees naturally respond to new ideas are influenced by many factors.

Spending time identifying where employees fall within the Diffusion of Innovation Model provides helpful understanding of how new ideas will be socially accepted, embraced, and ultimately adopted. Building a community of change agents will not happen overnight, yet strategically leveraging specific employee strengths can significantly impact the rest of your team.

Personal Reactions

Understanding how we naturally react to new information is especially beneficial to mindfully introducing change. Each person you lead has specific needs based on their experiences, personalities, and emotions. A person's existing knowledge and experiences impact how they perceive and interpret new information. In this case, let's explore what happens when an employee is presented with a new idea.

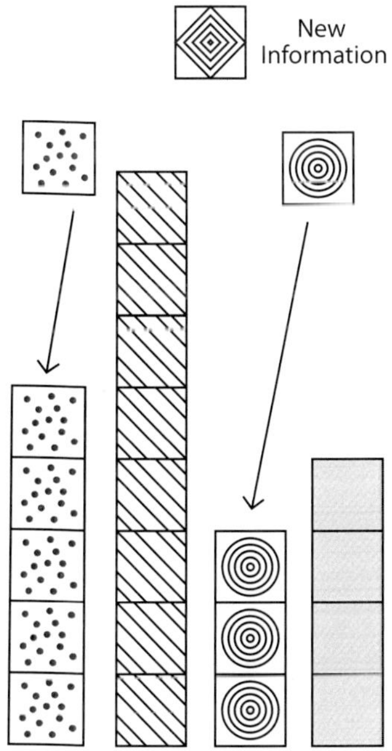

I like to envision that we have several pillars of knowledge in our minds. As we grow up, we are exposed to new experiences and observations which give us information that we file away as knowledge. Now imagine that each piece of information is a building block that we categorize by stacking it with other, similar information. This begins to form a pillar of knowledge. As similar information is accumulated and stacked upon one another, our knowledge becomes more and more affirmed. Any time we encounter new information, we naturally try to categorize it within our existing pillars of knowledge. Put simply, we compare new information with previous context and experience to try and understand it. Doing so helps us know how we need to respond to this new information. What would happen if you were exposed to something completely new that you couldn't fit into any of those categories of knowledge? While it seems simple to just create a new pillar, people are actually met with an immediate struggle or dissonance and they often aren't sure how to react. This can be very jarring for some.

What does this mean for us? When presenting employees with new software, we must consider how they are making meaning of this new solution. They will likely attempt to categorize the new tool into an existing knowledge pillar. For some they may make sense of it by comparing it to previous software they have used. This could lead them to question how the new software is different than those they have used in the past. For others, they may understand it as a replacement for a manual process. This might lead to questions about whether or not the new software can truly accomplish what the manual process did. For a few, they may not even be able to find meaning in the new software at all. With everyone's pillars of knowledge being unique, there is not a one-size-fits-all approach.

Although people may not interpret newly presented information the same way, leaders can help them understand how the new software fits within their existing knowledge pillars. This is best accomplished by providing context, offering comparisons, and using analogies. For example, while explaining a new Customer Relationship Management solution (CRM), you could describe it as, "Software that has a searchable customer directory, like your own digital address book." When comparing the new software to a similar tool, you could say, "This new CRM is similar to our email contact list, but offers additional features to automate emails and messages." Explaining how the new software fits within their existing knowledge structure will guide your employees through reluctance and mitigates discomfort that is brought forth with change.

Assessing Employee Needs

Let's dive deeper into the psychology of how change affects people. My mentor once told me that change is a grieving process and we need to make sure that we're treating it as such. Take a moment and think about that statement: change is a grieving process. What is your initial reaction? Do you agree or disagree?

Change is always accompanied by loss. No matter how big or small, grief is a strong and sometimes overwhelming emotion and can't be overlooked. Yet we often think the best way to get people on board with change is to "win them over" through enthusiasm and sharing more information. If you were experiencing grief and I said to you:

"We have this new software, it will be so exciting! We are so eager to use it, we can't wait! It's going to make your work five times easier and faster. You can add customers, keep track of emails, send messages, create workflows, build reports... You should sign up for training right away. It's going to be awesome!"

I'm guessing you would feel a little overwhelmed, right? This is probably the last thing you would want to hear while experiencing loss. When we try to "sell" change, we are skipping over the entire grieving process and your employees will quickly feel cornered. How do we often react when cornered? That's right, fight or flight. When people are confronted with change, their sense of stability could be threatened because they are losing what they had before. To combat this, we need to put just as much, if not more, energy into navigating employee emotions than navigating the change itself.

How someone perceives change is truly in the eye of the beholder. Each person reacts to change differently and an event is only viewed as a "transition" if the individual believes that it will change their relationships, routines, assumptions, and/or roles (Schlossberg 2008). Some employees, like the early adopters for example, may not view the implementation of new software as a transition. Some of the later adopters may to varying degrees. Everyone's perception of the change is valid and we'll need to be prepared for the full gamut of human emotions that may accompany the transition.

Although endless research on the emotions experienced during change is available, I am partial to John Fisher's

Personal Transition Curve. Fisher's model is comprehensive and takes into account the variety of emotions people experience when navigating change (2012). This model can help us understand the consequences of change so we can provide our employees with support while the change takes place. The curve shown in Fisher's model illustrates both the high and the low emotions that people go through when change is present. The degree to which each emotion is experienced differs for each employee based on their circumstances at the time.

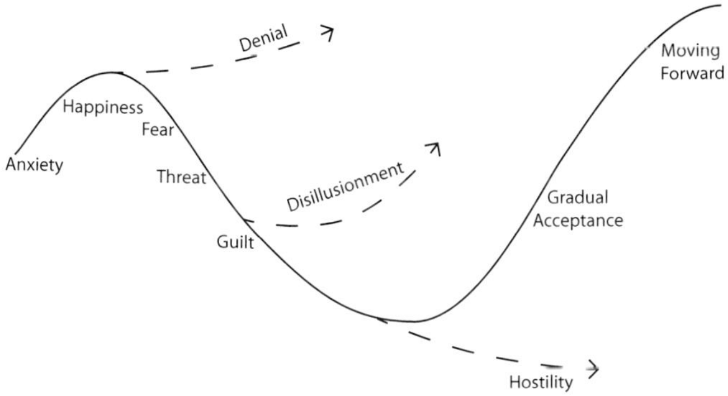

Adapted from Personal Transition Curve (Fisher 2012).

Anxiety, happiness, denial, fear, threat, guilt, depression, hostility, gradual acceptance, delusionment, and moving forward are just scratching the surface of the emotional experience associated with change. To know that we are presented with endless change every day, to varying degrees of course, makes it so clear why additional change can be met with feelings other than excitement. Remember, it is our role to consider how change may affect our employees and to be proactive in mitigating yet another emotional rollercoaster.

Managing multiple reactions to change is potentially a big undertaking. While your employees may naturally respond to change in various ways, there are common needs that each employee will have throughout the transition. Nancy Schlossberg, a transition expert and founder of the Schlossberg Transition Theory, helps us understand the essential needs of our employees and encourages us to "take stock" on how each of them will handle the rollout of new software by assessing four key variables.

Situation

What are the circumstances of the transition? Will the change result in a change of role or responsibilities? How might the timing of this change impact the employee's perception of it? What level of control does this employee have during the transition process? Is this employee capable of handling this load?

Self

Who is immediately impacted by this change? To what degree will the change impact them? What abilities and skills do they have to navigate the transition? What is their outlook within the organization?

Support

What resources does this employee have access to? How can the resources guide and support their transition? Is their interpersonal network offering positive, negative, or neutral support? Is this employee aware of the support systems available?

Strategies

What coping mechanisms does this employee have that can help them manage a transition? How have they used these coping mechanisms in the past to mitigate feelings of overwhelm and stress?

Consider each employee's ability to cope with the transition to new software by walking through this list of variables. Determine the areas which are sufficient or "positive" and which may be lacking or "negative". The positive areas are assets and can be counted on to benefit your employees' transition. The negative areas will require more attention and perhaps even intervention to prepare your employees for the transition.

One way to manage employee emotions during change is to engage them in the process itself. Leaders who spend time understanding the impact of change on their employees will be able to foster increased levels of engagement. I value the power of the "collective whole" to navigate and adopt new software. Including several perspectives in the change process fosters a kinetic energy and motivation that drives productive change within the entire organization. Take advantage of every opportunity to involve employees while ensuring everyone feels heard and valued. This is best achieved by determining specific stages of the change process that would benefit from their input. Active engagement fuels employees' investment in a common vision and the feeling that they are making a significant contribution toward the growth of the organization. This increases a sense of ownership and drive toward a successful outcome while contributing to a more robust organization that reflects multiple perspectives.

4 Define Your Role in Change

"If you are entrusted with bringing about change, you likely possess the knowledge needed to advance the organization, and you might have a plan—but knowledge is not enough. You have to bring yourself to each interaction in a deeply authentic way. People don't care how much you know until they know how much you care."

- Doug Conant

Transforming an organization depends more heavily on leadership than management. Far too often those at the helm of an organization focus more on managing change than on leading an organization through change. Management includes planning, budgeting, resource allocation, establishing policies and procedures, and delegating. Leadership prepares, guides, and responds to the organizational transformation and adoption of change. While change management and organizational leadership are both essential during the change process, the success of change truly boils down to the people that will drive it forward. As a leader, it is your job to ensure the change process is moving forward with clarity and conviction. Your role is multifaceted and requires unique attention given to your employees' experience.

Leader Disposition

Leaders must be humbly devoted to understanding themselves, their team, and their organization. Their interest in personal growth and development encourages growth in others. The first step in leading change is to consider your personal disposition as you set out to lead others through the change process. Employees model after leaders when deciding norms, behaviors, and disposition. This modeling happens both intentionally and unintentionally. Therefore, employees will look to you for how to react and respond to change. Let's explore an example of the relationship between a toddler and their parent. Now, I am not saying that your employees are like small children, this is merely an example of leader and follower behavior. If a toddler is playing on the playground and has a minor fall, what is their first instinct? Some would say they might cry, yet I would disagree. Their first instinct is to look at their parent to gauge whether or not they should cry. If the parent immediately reacts with a grimace and quickly reaches to scoop them up, the toddler will most likely begin crying. On the other hand, if the parent quickly evaluates the child to ensure they are uninjured and carries on with what they were doing; the child will often stand up, brush off any dirt, and continue playing. This concept can be translated to your leader and follower relationship. When an employee is faced with a challenging or jarring situation, they will often observe you to gauge how they should react. Awareness of how you are perceived by employees will help you adjust your disposition to positively model and influence their reactions to change. Let's use the analogy of "acting like a duck." Appear calm and collected above the surface, but paddle like mad below. Now is a great time to pause and assess the following factors.

Your current state of mind. Are you in a state of panic or stress? How could that be perceived by your employees if not kept in check? Perceiving emotional balance in a leader throughout the change process cultivates employee confidence and instills trust that the change is not only necessary, but also achievable without undue stress.

Your motivation for the change. Are you feeling pressure from external sources? Will that pressure be passed down to your employees? Employees can easily sense if their leader is experiencing pressure from above. While you may be feeling this strain, mitigating the trickle-down effect onto your employees will shield them from feeling overwhelmed and give them emotional space to navigate change.

Personal agendas that could impact the change. Is this change important to the entire organization and employees or is it more advantageous for you? Personal agendas are easy to spot by employees as they are used to observing and assessing your every move. If even a hint of a personal agenda is perceived, your employees will be less motivated to contribute to the change process, or in this case, adopt a new software system.

The urgency of the change. How quickly are you trying to implement your software? Is the timeline realistic and will it cause unnecessary stress on your employees? Setting your team up for success can make or break the change process. If you have a quick implementation timeline,

I encourage you to ask yourself, "Why so fast?" Could it be that your excitement is taking precedence over ensuring your employees have a positive experience through the change process?

By evaluating your current disposition as the leader of change, you are already beginning the process with intentionality and humility. This awareness will help you understand your impact on employees as you navigate the entire process. Change is accompanied by many emotions, as we will discuss in subsequent chapters, and balancing your own personal constitution will offer stability for your employees.

Set the Vision

Leaders create vision for their followers. While we know communicating the vision for your organization as a whole is a critical component of leadership, communicating the vision for change is just as important. Anytime you set out to reach a goal, you need a vision, so all people affected can see and understand where you are going. For instance, let's say you were planning to introduce a new system to help manage your business, simply saying, "We have new software that you'll start using at the end of the month," leaves your employees with uncertainty and plenty of questions. This can be a jarring experience. Instead, include the vision in your statement. For example, "We will begin to use a new software program that will help us get more organized and increase productivity so that we can eliminate the miscommunication that we're experiencing."

An effective vision maximizes potential while remaining achievable. Stretch your vision just beyond reach to challenge your team, while ensuring they have the right support to feel confident in their ability to reach it. Balance within a vision will give followers purpose and motivate them toward the flicker of light at the end of the tunnel. A leader must also remain flexible. While you may have a vision for the change, your employees could have other ideas that can inform the overall vision. If you shut their ideas down, you will risk losing any motivation they had for seeing the change through. Stifling their excitement is a surefire way to cause resistance.

Create the Strategy

Creating a strategy for change ensures your ducks are in a row and this requires you to take a step back. Evaluate your organization's current state and then create a transition plan for moving through the change process. I'm sure we can all think of leaders who get all too excited about new initiatives and it may even seem like they push for change every day. I'll be the first to admit I have impacted my own employees in this way. As someone who is future-thinking and idea-driven, I come up with new ideas practically every minute! Initially, I was extremely excited to share and implement these ideas, but then I noticed my employees were beginning to feel overwhelmed. The constant stream of ideas and change interrupted their work and ability to effectively prioritize their tasks. I had to make a conscious decision to filter my ideas before sharing them and be selective in those I chose to implement. While it was extremely difficult to reign in my enthusiasm, I created a rule for myself: new ideas or change could not be introduced until I developed a strategy for them. The first step was creating an "idea journal" through a notes app on my phone. Unlike a physical notebook, my phone would always be within arm's reach when an idea struck. I simply added any new thought or idea to this journal with as much detail as possible at the time. One hour each week was set aside for me to review the ideas from the week prior and give each a simple rating based on how much value it could add if implemented. This exercise distinguished between mere ideas and possible changes that had the potential to make a significant impact. Once identified, more time and attention could be given to the ideas that had the highest rating. For each idea, I considered:

- The positive and negative side effects of the change.
- How the change could align with the broader organizational vision.
- The resources needed to carry the change forward.
- Where this change would land among my team's existing priorities.

By following the rule, I sift through my constant flow of ideas and am selective with those I choose to explore further. I could also be methodical in my approach when sharing the ideas with my team. This one seemingly simple switch not only gave my employees more clarity and consistency, it also increased their confidence in me as a leader because I had my act together.

Sometimes we get ahead of ourselves, don't have a strategy ironed out, or maybe our enthusiasm pushes change too fast. Frequent changes without strategy could result in our employees being in a constant state of ambiguity. Eventually, we could even cause the "boy who cried wolf" phenomenon where employees stop taking action after a change is communicated, just to wait and see if the idea will stick. This halts all productivity. It is important that we establish defined steps to prepare for change. Not just at the leadership level, but also establish steps for each employee to take when the change is presented. As a leader, be proactive and consider the impact of the change on each of your employees. How will the change affect their roles and responsibilities? I like to think of myself as an "undercover boss" where I put myself in each of my employees' shoes and imagine all the possible ways the change could affect them. How might they need to prepare for the change? Is there anything you can do now that would ease the burden or stress on them when you introduce the change? What reactions can you anticipate so you are always one step ahead of your team? I'm glad we've got your wheels spinning as we will continue exploring specific methods for creating change strategies in later chapters.

Keep an Eye on Culture

Tune into the culture and pay particular attention to the attitudes and dispositions of your employees before, during, and after the change process. This means keeping your finger on the pulse of your organization. Everyone is an influencer in your organization whether they are the business owner, manager, administrator, or any other role; they all influence the thought process of others. You may be leading the new software implementation, and your role may put you in a position to hold different responsibilities than others, yet you alone cannot drive team adoption. Know who you need in your corner to achieve the results you are hoping for.

I remember thinking it would be easy to rally employees around a change simply because it was the most logical path to reach our goals. However, what I didn't prepare for was my employees having side conversations without me in the room to add my perspective and share my logic. I've always encouraged my employees to speak with one another and build one-on-one relationships, so as a leader, I should have anticipated these "off the record" conversations. As they spoke with one another, a seed of doubt spread throughout the team and concerns started bubbling up. Unbeknownst to me, my employees planned how to collectively share their concerns during an upcoming meeting and it completely caught me off guard. Not only was I ill-prepared to help my team navigate their concerns, but we had to rethink the change altogether. People seek understanding of new concepts through social interactions with others. If an employee's resistance or negativity is overlooked, it could derail your entire change strategy. Be aware of nonverbal cues, attitudes, and perceptions of your employees so you can address them as they arise rather than hoping they will somehow disappear.

Also, identify employees who understand the change and create coalitions that can help communicate the purpose of the change with others in your organization. These "project champions" can keep you informed of the state of your culture and the direction it is heading. Those who believe in the "why" behind the change will drum up support and be eager to share that vision throughout the organization. This provides a positive trickle effect that is necessary to keep the culture balanced and moving forward. Without positive influence, negativity could permeate throughout the culture and create an uphill battle. Who are your project champions?

- Which employees seem to embrace change and show an eagerness to explore new possibilities?
- Who on your team carries significant influence among others?
- Is there anyone who is vocal about challenges and concerns in which this change might benefit?

Involve Stakeholders

Let's determine our audience. To whom do we need to justify the purpose of this change? I like to call this identifying our stakeholders. A stakeholder is a key person or group that has high interest or concern in your organization, its actions, or decisions (in this case, the new software). Stakeholders include those who can influence the change or might be influenced by the change. It really only takes a few key stakeholders to completely hijack your change efforts, so identifying them up front prepares you to get ahead of any obstacles that could interfere with their support for the change.

Some examples of key stakeholders in organizations include supervisors, department or division leaders, leadership teams, and of course, the chief officers. Stakeholders could also include entry level employees who are influential to others in the organization. Take a few moments to write down who your stakeholders are. Who makes decisions within your organization? Who will decide the funding for the new software? Who tends to influence others on your team? Who must be involved in the implementation to make it run smoothly? This list will tell us the people that we need to communicate with early to justify the purpose of the new software.

Stakeholders:

1. ______________________________
2. ______________________________
3. ______________________________
4. ______________________________
5. ______________________________

It is also important to remember that not all stakeholders are equal—as we know, some have a stronger voice than others. Circle or highlight your stakeholders who have the most potential to influence the success of the change. Sometimes these are not simply the highest position in a hierarchy. They could be the technology staff, department managers, or even the software users. Really think about who has the power of influence. Those who you have highlighted will need the highest level of involvement throughout the software implementation. Gaining initial stakeholder buy-in and maintaining their support throughout the implementation will mitigate obstacles you are bound to face during the change process.

Now that you have spent time reflecting on your role while encouraging team adoption during the implementation process, we can begin exploring the nuts and bolts of how to best introduce the change. Countless leaders have told me they wish they would have introduced new software to their team differently. In hindsight they recognized that approaching the change more methodically would have saved them headaches down the road. They also shared that the change process would have been much quicker if they planned ahead. Let's save ourselves from any regrets by planning the introduction of the change with our employees at the forefront.

5 Build a Case for Change

"The people must have ownership in the vision. They need to be enabled to accomplish it. If there is one investment you should make, it is in people."

– Modesta Lilian Mbughuni

After deciding to embark on this new endeavor, it is time to build a case for the change so it has a strong foundation. Creating the "why" or underlying purpose for the change will give it backing and support throughout the process. In an ideal world, the purpose for change would be identified collectively by your entire team, so all of your employees can align with it. Yet, in some cases, leadership may establish the core purpose of the change and you'll need to ensure all employees fully understand the "why" behind it. The following sections provide several exercises that will help you build a case for implementing new software. Download a free workbook to put these exercises into practice from my website: www.anna-hunter.com/book.

To achieve successful adoption of change, it is critical that we start the conversation early. If you ask me "how early is too early?" I would say never. If you ask me "when is the best time to discuss change with my team?" I would say today. Now, remember to keep your enthusiasm in check and begin the conversation with strategy and careful intent. You do not need to have all the answers at this point, in fact it is better if you don't! The more malleable you can be when discussing change, the easier it will be to invite employees into the conversation. You are simply inspiring conversation about the need for change, not details about what the change will be or how it might look. A common misconception is that leaders need to have a polished plan to present new software to their employees. However, by the time you feel "ready," it will be too late, resulting in higher chances of your employees responding with reluctance and resistance. Consider your own feelings when a new idea is pushed upon you and it feels like it came out of left field. Isn't it even more alarming when you didn't realize there was a need for change?

Everyone wants to feel like they matter and are valued. Inviting them into the conversation early communicates that they are just as critical to the success of the change as everyone else in the organization (which they are!). In fact, the sooner you discuss the need for change, the sooner your employees will bring themselves through the emotional journey that accompanies change. Would you rather have them respond with emotionally-charged reactions and lean on you to guide them through each emotion? If so, then you have a long, treacherous road ahead. The more your employees are informed, the less uncertainty they experience throughout the process. Well-informed organizations have the most potential for effective communication and overall growth. While transparency is key, remember, you do not need to have all the answers to prepare your team for the change process. Rather, work toward four goals to build a case for the change:

1. Clarify the current issues
2. Communicate underlying consistency
3. Build consensus around priorities
4. Commit to resolving the problem

These four goals for early conversations will provide a soft opening to bring your employees on board at the very beginning. Later on, when you are encouraging them to actually use the new tool, it'll be a lot easier. At this time, you may not have chosen the specific software solution yet. All you need to worry about now is setting your team up for success. Let's take a deep dive into each goal to effectively build a case for introducing the new software to your employees.

Clarify the Current Issues

Help your employees see the cause-and-effect relationship of the current, ineffective system. Then explain why a change needs to happen. Don't get into the weeds about the exact change, simply make a case for why you can't continue moving forward with your current systems. Use the following statement as a guide:

> "We are currently doing ______ *(insert current process here)* ______, which is resulting in ______ *(insert ineffective result of the current process here)* ______. It is impacting our ability to achieve our vision and goals."

Communicating the current problem positions employees in a solution-oriented state of mind that breeds thoughts about possibility. This reduces hesitancy and disarms the change process.

Pinpoint the Need for Change

Organizations are inherently "simple" when they originate. Yet over time, leaders attempt to increase effectiveness by introducing new processes, procedures, personnel, and you guessed it…software. This often results in convoluted systems and complicated structures. Rarely do organizations step back to review, reduce, and streamline systems in an effort to simplify operations. Yet it is important to strike a proper balance between complexity and simplicity. Doing so will ultimately benefit the organization as a whole.

Before embarking on the change process, make clear the reason why you are considering introducing a new software solution and how it will fit within the greater organizational system. Most likely, you are bringing it on to assist with ineffective processes. There could be so many other reasons like creating efficiencies, adapting to internal changes, meeting new expectations of customers, optimizing practices, fostering sustainability and growth, or simply adding overall value to the organization. If you can relate to any of these reasons, then the next exercise will be valuable for you.

Leverage Process Mapping

A great way to clarify the need for new software is by evaluating your existing processes and identifying how they are falling short. Process mapping provides a visual display of the steps within a process and serves as a powerful tool to justify the need for change. Let's walk through this exercise together. The key steps of process mapping for improvement are listed below.

1. Process Mapping: Outline the inner workings of the process

2. Analysis: Identify gaps, redundancies, bottlenecks, inefficiencies, etc.

3. Ask Questions: Evaluate the process from an internal and external point of view

Use any medium you would like to create your process map. Some use a whiteboard, others use a simple pen and paper, and many use online diagramming tools. Any of those methods can be just as effective. The goal is to produce a step-by-step flow of the entire process, from start to finish. You can choose to be as detailed or high-level as you would like, as long as you include primary steps and any significant secondary steps. Also, make note of any handoffs, where information or tasks are traveling between people as well as feedback loops where steps within the process are revisited. Here is an example of a process map that illustrates a sales pipeline.

Now, I encourage you to take a moment to begin creating your process map. Choose a particular workflow in your

organization that will most likely be impacted by the new software, whether that be sales, account management, cash flow, employee onboarding, etc. Start by listing at least five sequential steps in your existing workflow. What are the steps that you currently take to get from point A to point B? Now that you have a head start, go ahead and continue mapping out the rest of your current process. You may notice some inefficiencies in your process already, but refrain from getting caught up on them right now; simply continue mapping out your process as-is.

Once you have mapped your process, it is time to begin the map analysis. Before we can confidently determine that new software is truly going to improve our process, we need to evaluate and clean up our existing steps. Initially, try to find ways to optimize the workflow. Begin by highlighting steps that can be combined, run concurrently, be automated, or simplified. These are opportunities for improving your process. Next, identify and cross out areas to reduce or eliminate duplicate information, unnecessary handoffs, delays, and approval tiers. These changes can create efficiencies within your process.

The next phase of the map analysis is to cut down resources. Minimize steps that do not add value. Steps that can often be removed are prevention steps, appraisal steps, and steps added to temporarily fix failures. Here are a few questions to ask as you are assessing each step:

- What value does this step add?
- Which stakeholder benefits from this step?

- Does our customer care enough to use our resources in this way?
- What do we already have in place that can support us with this?

The final phase in the map analysis is to rethink the current steps altogether. Identify what "should be" versus what "could be." Challenge the outcome of the process and then determine if the current steps are actually helping you reach the desired outcome. Think about which steps might be based on tradition and are holding you back from progress. Ask the following questions:

- What are we looking to accomplish or create?
- Is this still required by all stakeholders?
- What is stopping us from eliminating this step?
- How many steps does each internal and external user need to take?
- Do we really need this step? What would happen if we didn't have it?
- Why not try something different?

Once you have analyzed your map, it is time to recreate your ideal workflow by illustrating how the process should look once you implement a new software system. This map will hopefully be more streamlined and efficient, therefore providing clear justification for the new software and can help communicate the intent of the change. In order for your employees to trust future change, they must see that this new solution will truly add value to their roles and the broader organization rather than adding more work. Avoid workarounds. If you are adding new software to temporarily patch a failure within your process, then I encourage you to dig deeper and seek out the root cause of the issue. Then choose a solution that will truly fix the real problem. Otherwise, you will be in this very same position again in a few months. Showing a clear, visual comparison between what you are currently doing and what "could be" can garner buy-in from your employees as well as stakeholders. Process mapping simply makes the need for change undeniable.

Communicate Underlying Consistency

Leading through change requires a balance between development and maintenance. Maintaining a degree of consistency provides a foundation upon which change can thrive. An essential component of change management is giving your employees a constant they can cling to if they are feeling off balance. As I grew up on construction sites and moved from job to job on a frequent basis, the constant I clung to was a tire swing that my dad hung at each job site. Just a simple old tire and rope gave me the stability I needed to navigate daily inconsistency. In order to navigate change, followers must feel a connection to an origin or a constant throughout the change. Leaders can accomplish this by including followers in the change process and valuing their need for a level of stability. Determine how you will provide consistency that your employees can count on throughout the change process to reduce uncertainty. Always explain what you are planning to happen as a result of the change and that will help employees buy into its purpose. Then communicate exactly what they can depend on and follow through on this promise. An organization's mission, vision, and values provide a North Star for your team.

> **Mission**
>
> A mission provides a purpose that will girdle all emotions experienced by employees. It roots them in the "why" and provides stability that will sustain them through uncertainty.
>
> **Vision**
>
> Being a part of a vision that is greater than oneself arms employees with confidence in decisions made by leadership, specifically that any change endured is contributing toward a greater goal.
>
> **Values**
>
> Employees often cling to organizational values alongside their inner compass to feel centered. Centering oneself provides safety upon which one can take risks.

Balance in vision gives your employees a purpose and a foundation upon which to grow. Have you ever experienced an earthquake first-hand? One minute you are going about your day and all is normal. Then the next minute, the ground you have always counted on for stability and security is suddenly no longer stable. It is an incredibly disorienting feeling that causes you to immediately search for something you can depend on to feel secure again. After all, the phrase "feeling grounded" assumes the ground serves as a stable, reliable foundation. To mitigate feelings of disruption and instability, align your new software to the greater purpose of your organization so your employees feel grounded as they experience inconsistencies that arise during the change process. Providing elements of consistency that remain undisturbed during change will give your employees confidence in your ability to lead them through the process and it would be risky to break this trust. Now, how do we create a connection between the new software and our organization's vision, mission, and values to give our employees the stability they need? We can accomplish this through a simple alignment exercise.

Align Software to a Greater Purpose

We can start by gathering a "big picture" of what we are trying to accomplish. Locate your organization's guiding principles, such as the mission, vision, values, and goals. Let's call these collectively our organization's "purpose." All change within your organization should connect to the greater purpose. This inverted triangle diagram illustrates the relationship between our organizational purpose, any department purposes, and the purpose of the new software. Now each organization has various levels within its hierarchy, so you can add layers to this. We'll keep it relatively simple by discussing three levels.

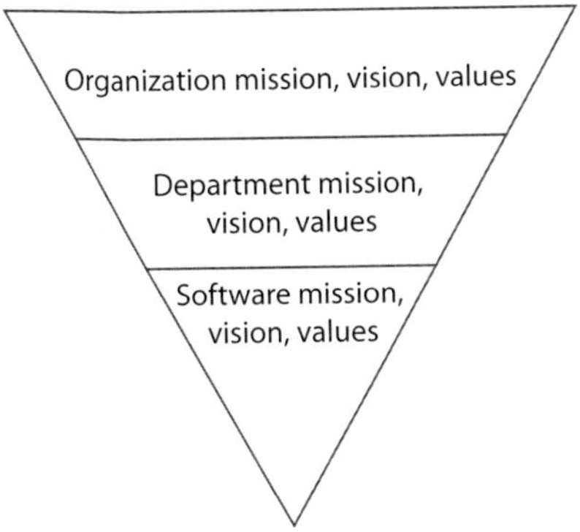

We will work from the top down showing the connection between a department's purpose and the organization's purpose. Furthermore, we should be able to define the purpose of the new software in a way that aligns with both the department and the organization. In doing so, we can demonstrate that the solution directly supports the organization's purpose. Ask yourself, how can we link the new software to the purposes overhead? What words are used within the organization and department vision, mission, and values that could also apply to your vision with the software? How can you write the software vision, mission, and goals in a way that directly connects to the broader organization?

Aligning the vision for your new software with the greater purpose of your organization will provide your employees with stability and add further justification for the change. Justification should show that introducing the new software within your organization is the most "reasonable" or "sensible" decision. Without the new solution, we would be missing out on an opportunity to support the organization's mission.

Build Consensus Around Priorities

Generate agreement around the fact that you currently have a problem and something does need to change. Your employees don't necessarily need to know how the problem will be solved or what the exact steps are for the change process. In fact, they don't even need to know about the new software yet. Simply getting them on board with the fact that change does need to happen and agreeing on priorities as the change process is underway can provide reassurance and reduce unnecessary fear. Priorities could be based on the type, cost, usability, or accessibility of the chosen software, minimal impact to current employee roles and responsibilities, maintenance of existing workflows, etc. Imagine how relieved you would feel if you had the chance to express your fears and concerns regarding an upcoming change. What if you were even invited to help determine priorities of the outcome? I know I would feel incredibly valued and at ease...heck, maybe even excited about what is to come! Building consensus around the priorities that will remain paramount during the change will ease tension and give people comfort through the process. Priorities should be outlined in our goals.

Create Goals for the Change

What do you want to achieve as a result of this change? What are the intended effects of implementing new software? Let's create goals for the change that are directly linked to its vision. A goal is defined in broad terms and will be centered around the new software.

> **Formula:** A goal of (the software) is to (verb) (condition).

> **Example:** A goal of the new CRM is to increase customer acquisition.

Go ahead and try creating at least one goal now using the formula above. It can be helpful to align the goals for your new software with the company and/or department goals as well.

Let's go even one step further. Now that you have at least one goal for your new software system, let's create outcomes, which are the action steps that inform our assessment. An outcome is the desired effect of a service or intervention, and provides specific steps that need to be completed to achieve a goal. It is participant- or output-centered. In other words, what the new software is to do, achieve, or accomplish.

> **Formula:** (Condition), (audience) will (behavior verb) (degree).

> **Example:** As a result of tracking the sales pipeline on the new CRM, sales managers will follow up with all leads within twenty-four hours.

The condition is how the software will be used, the audience is who will be participating, behavior is the future action we hope they will complete, and the degree is the minimum performance standard or the measurement.

See the example above and try one for yourself. Your outcomes should align directly with the goals of your new software. Establishing these goals now not only adds clarity for your employees, but also gives you specific parameters to adhere to as you are searching for the best software solution.

Commit to Resolving the Problem

Gain commitment to resolve the existing problem, regardless of what solution is chosen. Reassure employees that you will keep the agreed-upon priorities front and center while deciding on the best software solution. Verify that all employees support the idea of change and that they will do their best to make sure that the resolution is successful. When they agree with the change process, they will be bought into the end result.

Overcome Bureaucratic Barriers

Bureaucracy is everywhere and leaders, like you, are best positioned to overcome bureaucratic barriers so that your employees are not affected by them. You are essentially the buffer for your employees so they are protected from negative pressures and road blocks. Leaders typically have the drive to overcome barriers to change, especially when they are pushing for the change to take place. Your employees rarely have the same level of drive to persevere through barriers, so smoothing the path for them will not only reduce stress and frustration, but also affirms them of the change process. The path of least resistance is often necessary when guiding employees through uncharted waters.

Plan Assessment Measures

How will we know if the change is successful? This is a good time to start planning assessment measures that will give us confidence that the change is reaching the goals we set out for. It may seem too early to think about assessment, however, the best time to plan for assessment is before change takes place. Not only should we be thinking about what we are trying to achieve, we should also have a grasp on how we will know if we have achieved it. Ironing this out now gives you a chance to build in appropriate methods for tracking your progress before it becomes an afterthought. For example, you may need to set up specific reporting tools, live data streams, or surveys that will be referenced for data. Your change will also hold more credibility in the eyes of your employees if they know you have planned how to measure its success.

When designing your assessment plan, incorporate measures that assess the progress of the software adoption as well as those that assess whether the software is meeting its goals after it is implemented. It may also be helpful to incorporate a variety of methods and deliveries. I like to map out my assessment methods in a table format to add clarity while deciding the best strategy. Simply write your goal and/or outcome in the first column.

Desired Goal or Outcome	**Timing or Frequency**	**Assessment Method**	**Preparation and Needs**
As a result of tracking the sales pipeline on the new CRM, sales managers will follow up with all leads within twenty-four hours.	*Summative: Review quarterly*	*Reporting data: Calculate follow-up frequency per employee.*	*Live report showing percentages of response turnaround times for each sales employee.*

Next decide the timing of each assessment method. Which of your assessment measures are to be conducted during the implementation process to ensure that you are meeting training, onboarding, and adoption goals? This would be considered a *formative* assessment. Its purpose is to provide insights and feedback that can be used to shape, modify, or improve the implementation before it is complete. Formative assessment methods are also commonly used to track progress toward meeting the goals of the new software within the first year of implementation so we can make tweaks and shift gears as we go. This could be as simple as check-ins during weekly staff meetings. *Summative* assessment is typically conducted after the implementation is complete, allowing us to make judgments on the quality and process so we can incorporate changes into future planning. Summative assessment can also be used to track milestones while the software is being used. Perhaps you have annual assessment cycles that align with your goals and you use summative assessment to review whether you met the goals or fell short.

Now you can decide the type of assessment you will use to measure each. Some common assessment methods that directly involve your employees include surveys, pre-test/post-test, quizzes, interviews, observation of skills, and self-reflection. Methods that leverage the gold mine of data provided by the software itself include anything you can report on such as employee usage through frequency of logins, user activity through the number of actions taken in the system, and of course aggregated data such as totals and quantities.

Lastly, identify anything you need to prepare in advance so you can properly capture the necessary data for your assessments. For example, do you need to create a pre-test to assess your team's current knowledge or productivity? Maybe you need to establish a baseline for current productivity to measure against once you implement the new software. Are there any reports that you should set up now that can be carried over to the new system? Success must be measured and preparing your assessment now will save plenty of headaches when you are in the thick of the implementation later!

Now that you have spent time intentionally introducing the idea of change to your team, you can confidently settle on the best software solution. Remember to keep your vision, goals, outcomes, and priorities front and center when exploring solutions to follow through on the promises you made with your employees! Once decided upon, you can begin guiding their adoption of the new software and work toward successful implementation.

6 Guide Change Adoption

"The tipping point is the magic moment when an idea, trend, or social behavior crosses a threshold, tips, and spreads like wildfire."

– Malcom Gladwell

When you are ready to share the new software solution you've decided on with your team, be prepared to walk them through an entire adoption process. It is also important to find a role for all people involved. I can't stress this enough. If people are involved, they will take ownership, see the change through, and remain committed to the end result. The goal is to foster intrinsic motivation and a commitment to the greater organization.

Stages of Adoption

Within his Diffusion of Innovations Framework, Everett Rogers (1962) describes five specific stages of the adoption process that are rooted in the psychology of how people respond to change. Completing all five steps is instrumental to successful change.

Knowledge → Persuasion → Decision → Implementation → Confirmation

Adapted from Five Stages in the Innovation-Decision Process (Rogers 1962).

Knowledge

Employees within this stage are exposed to the new software, but lack knowledge to make an informed opinion. The best approach here is to arm your employees with context and explain the vision for the change. Be sure to emphasize not only how the software will benefit the organization, but also how it will benefit each person in their respective roles. Create curiosity, but do not push at this stage! You are merely introducing the idea of the new solution, which may prompt them to look into it on their own.

Casually mention, "I found this new software and we are starting to look into it, I would be curious to know your thoughts." Then step away and let their curiosity take over. Asking this question takes less than ten seconds of your time and your employees will not only feel valued, but they will also feel as though they are part of the decision. Check back with them a couple of days later and listen to their thoughts. In most cases they are going to say some positive things about the software that you can cling to when moving to the persuasion stage.

Persuasion

Within this stage, your employees are showing an interest in the new software. Let's be clear, your goal is not to actively persuade them at this time. Rather your goal is to help them persuade themselves. Encourage your employees to embark on an educational journey so they choose to seek out more information from their own trusted sources. Invite your employees into the exploration process by asking them to look up online reviews of the software, watch videos, or even ask other colleagues outside your organization for their thoughts.

Next, ask your employees to share their findings with you. This will not only give them accountability while exploring, but it will also help your employees feel that they are an integral part of the change process and that their feedback matters. You'll also be able to gauge their initial reactions. If they are less than positive, you can intervene and then carefully guide them in a productive direction before their opinions are solidified. On the other hand, trying to persuade your employees with an announcement such as, "We are bringing on a new software application and it will be amazing for our team, a total game changer, you're going to love it!" can only result in one of two reactions: acceptance or reluctance. This approach asks for a polarized response and leaves very little room for an open mind!

Decision

The Decision stage is when your employees start weighing whether or not the software will be the right fit for them. They begin asking themselves questions such as, "Will this really help me or is it going to give me more work?" or "Is it worth it to commit to this transition right now?" Understandable, right? All of us are concerned about work piling up and implementing new software takes a lot of work. Not to mention the time needed to become trained and comfortable using the system.

You'll find your employees performing a cost-benefit analysis, comparing the advantages and disadvantages of the software itself and what it will be like to navigate the change process. They will decide at this stage whether they will adopt or reject the change. Therefore your role is to provide reassurance by re-highlighting the problems within the existing system that were identified during earlier change conversations. Follow this by asking *what if* questions that will focus conversations on the value of the change. For example, "Remember we agreed that our current processes aren't helping us reach our goals? What if this new software could help streamline our processes and save us time?" The goal here is to reposition the new software as the "light at the end of the tunnel."

Implementation

During the Implementation stage, employees have bought into the decision of the new software. Now they are trying to figure out what their role is in the implementation process. This is the *how* stage. I caution you to begin discussions about *how* the new software will be implemented before this stage! It is natural for us to begin thinking of the nuts and bolts of the implementation before this point, but that may overwhelm your employees quickly. During the Implementation stage they may ask questions such as, "How can I implement it in a way that will help me?" Or, "How can I use the new software to the best of its ability?" and "How is my position affected and what changes will I need to make?"

Give employees responsibilities during the configuration and implementation based on their unique strengths. Employees who use their natural strengths in their work have higher engagement levels. Perhaps you could have them beta-test parts of the software that you are configuring. Ask how they think it can be set up differently to make the process more seamless and less cumbersome. We can easily over-process our processes. Just remember, we don't know if a system is user-friendly without the user.

I encourage you to ask questions that prompt employees to consider not only the benefits of the software for their individual role, but how it is going to help the company as a whole. Doing so will inspire them to think beyond their role and identify how they fit within the bigger picture. Guiding employees to consider its use on a macro level will communicate that the software has a greater purpose, which leads to higher levels of commitment in the success of its implementation.

Confirmation

Lastly, during the Confirmation stage, employees finalize their opinion on implementing the new software and often explore the new tool to its full potential. This is an exciting milestone that we can't overlook! You have officially hooked them, but you need to continue feeding this enthusiasm so it doesn't burn out. Point your employees toward resources, guides, training, and communities that will expose them to the software's capabilities. Introducing them to several resources is critical during this stage because they can begin thinking more broadly, discovering more use cases for the solution, and envisioning all the possibilities it offers.

Even better, involve these employees in the implementation process. Giving employees responsibilities during the implementation process will instill a sense of ownership and they will be sure to see the implementation through. Ask them to complete tasks, such as making a list of what they need for implementing the software in their respective role and embedding it into their day-to-day responsibilities. Delegate employees to create an internal "help desk" or a virtual manual that is designed specifically for your organization's use cases. You could even ask them to create videos to train other team members. They will learn and build confidence when they speak about what they know. These employees will quickly become power users of the software, serving as direct resources for their colleagues.

Charge employees with discovering tips, tricks, and cool use cases in the software that they can share with other team members. Creating fun engagement will maintain high momentum and energy. Their commitment to the change can have a positive effect on other employees who have not yet reached this stage.

Each and every employee will navigate through these five stages at very different paces, so it's not something that you can walk your team through as a group. You will need to focus on each individual's needs. Leverage the Diffusion of Innovation Model (Rogers 1962) that was explored in chapter two to identify how each person might move through the stages and consider what their needs will be at each stage. For example, Laggards are going to need a bit more time during the exploration phase. Early adopters, on the other hand, might buzz right through to the end if they like it. The Innovators might already be exploring how the new software can fit in everyone's role before you can even catch up! It's important that you truly consider what each person in your organization needs and to be ready for them to spend different amounts of time through each stage.

7 Navigate Resistance

"The announcement is the easy part; it makes the manager look bold and decisive. Implementation is more difficult, because no matter how good and compelling the data, there will always be active and passive resistance, rationalizations, debates, and distractions—particularly when the changes require new ways of working or painful cuts. To get through this, managers have to get their hands dirty, engage their teams to make choices, and sometimes confront recalcitrant colleagues."

– Ron Ashkenas and Rizwan Khan

In speaking with a close colleague, I learned about her firsthand experience as an employee navigating a pretty rough software transition. She worked in an information technology department with several others who also understood and appreciated the power of technology. The department had successfully used a ticketing system for several years. Yet, due to employee turnover, the system inputs and automations were not maintained as needed. Rather than seeking out the root cause of the issue, organizational leadership assumed the software was failing to meet the department needs. Shortly thereafter, an announcement was made that the department would switch to a completely different out-of-the-box software solution. As you can imagine, the employees felt blind-sided, disregarded, and unheard. Even after they attempted to share concerns through appropriate chains of command, leadership stuck with their decision and never offered an opportunity to hear directly from the employees themselves. When people aren't offered a safe space to speak about their frustrations with leadership, their only option is to voice frustrations with one another. In this case, heated "water-cooler" conversations between employees fueled feelings of distrust and defeat, which permeated throughout the department's culture. Several found alternative employment while those who did stick around were disengaged, only completing the minimum work required of them. The organization is still feeling the impact of this change several years later while attempting to recover from a polarized culture of "us versus them," rebuilding trust between leadership and the employees. In this case, leadership was trying to solve a problem, but did not choose to value the people behind the software and fully understand the source of the issue. Although their entire department worked in technology and was familiar with software transitions, the approach to the change resulted in widespread resistance.

Resistance is the failure to accept or comply with a change, and in this case adopting the new software. You may notice employees withdrawing, avoiding, disengaging, or rejecting the change altogether. In some cases, resistance can lead to attempts of undermining or sabotaging change efforts. Pretending resistance does not exist won't make it disappear. I've found ten underlying reasons why people often resist change and each of them are fear-based. Fear is not one-size-fits-all. It is perceived differently by everyone and presents itself in varying degrees. How we interpret fear is based on experiences, observations, and knowledge. While some of the fears listed below might seem irrational to you, they are very legitimate for others. Exploring each of them equips leaders with a clearer understanding of the extent of employee reactions as they are responding to change. Each is followed by common needs that employees have when experiencing the fear.

1. **Fear of Direct Change**

   Some individuals have low tolerance to change, which could result in anxiety when facing new experiences. Leaders often mistake employees as having a fear of direct change when they show any signs of reluctance. Yet this is far from the truth as each person has varying fears that contribute to their reactions. So be cautious not to assume your employees are experiencing this type of fear!

   Needs**:** Reassurance of what will remain consistent during the change process so they have something to count on.

2. **Fear of Reorganization**

   Some have a fear that this change will disturb the status quo and that it will force them out of their comfort zone.

Needs: Affirmation that they will have access to necessary resources and be supported throughout the change process.

3. **Fear of Loss**

   This fear is rooted in the concern that they are going to lose something of value as a result of the change. As you can imagine, this fear drives most of the grieving process experienced by those navigating change.

   Needs: Time to adjust to the loss, discussions about how they will navigate through the process at each stage, and expectations of how their work will look after the change.

4. **Fear of Implications**

   Some may not understand what will happen as a result of the change. Therefore they feel as though they are "walking off a cliff blindfolded."

   Needs: Context that explains why the change is taking place and communication regarding the vision for the change. Describe how the change fits within the larger vision of the organization.

5. **Fear of Uselessness**

   This fear is driven by the belief that the proposed change does not make sense for the organization. Therefore, it is unnecessary and happening for no reason.

***Needs*:** Insight into the failures of the existing system and understanding how the new software is a better solution.

6. **Fear of Loss of Control**

   Many people feel that change is exciting when it is carried out by them, but threatening when it is done to them. You may be surprised by their reluctance since they have shown excitement for change they've introduced in the past. However, if they do not feel in control of the change, they could be concerned by it.

   ***Needs*:** Involvement in the change process early on as well as defined responsibilities throughout the transition process.

7. **Fear of Losing Face**

   This fear stems from a belief that by going along with the new change, they are accepting that their previous decisions and processes were wrong. Inherently, they resist change to remain consistent with the past.

   ***Needs*:** Validation and recognition of what they have done in the past given the knowledge and resources they had at the time.

8. **Fear of Surprise**

   When change is suddenly announced, most people are so shocked that they would rather resist or undermine the change than accept it.

   ***Needs*:** Early transparency and involvement in discussions about change before the details of the change are decided upon.

9. **Fear of the Unknown**

   Some people are afraid of what will happen if they go through change. This is especially true if there is limited information provided and employees do not trust those leading the change.

   ***Needs*:** Information showing that maintaining the status quo is more dangerous than launching into the unknown.

10. **Fear of Threat**

    This fear presents itself when employees feel their position or work is threatened. If the new software will streamline or automate a process, they may be concerned that their role will not be as valuable to the organization. In turn, the change threatens their job security.

    ***Needs*:** Clearly defined post-change responsibilities and assurance that they will remain a valuable asset within the organization.

Each of these fears is valid in their own right and it is completely natural for one or multiple fears to trigger immediate reactions to change. The degree of each fear and the way in which it influences employees' reactions will vary, so please refrain from making assumptions about their reactions. Instead, put your agenda to the side and position yourself to tune into their emotional experiences so you can gain genuine empathy for their reactions. Only then will you understand how to respond so your employees will feel validated and choose to follow your lead.

Reluctance vs. Resistance

To avoid misreading an employee's reaction to the new software, let's explore the difference between reluctance and resistance. Reluctance is an unwillingness, a disinclination that is often an immediate, instinctual reaction. A common reason for reluctance is when new information doesn't fit within a person's existing knowledge pillars. An inability to instantly understand or make meaning of new information using previous knowledge creates skepticism and often reluctance.

Let's imagine that you are leading a meeting while standing in front of a conference room. One of your employees is standing six feet to your left. You ask them to stand closer to lessen the gap. After they take a half step closer to you, you ask them again to step closer. You continue until they are standing nearly shoulder-to-shoulder with you. Now, initially they probably did not think much of taking small steps closer, but as they were continually asked to close the gap, they probably became skeptical of the purpose of doing so, started questioning your intentions, and maybe even wondered what would happen if they said no and stood their ground. I'm sure we can agree that these are all natural reactions in this situation. This natural inclination to question whether to act when not given clarity is reluctance.

Let's continue so we gain a deeper understanding of reluctance. Next you ask them to stand shoulder-to-shoulder with you for the duration of the meeting. Some common reactions may include:

Indifference

The person may be completely fine with the request and confidently stand shoulder-to-shoulder without question. This shows that they are adapting to uncertainty really well. In this case, they might trust your intentions and respond with indifference.

Skepticism

The person may respond by leaning or taking a small step away from you; widening the gap a bit to feel more comfortable. In this case, they are not necessarily reluctant, but they are somewhat weary or unsure. We can work with this; they just need more information and more time.

Reluctance

The employee may move closer to their original position, perhaps uncomfortably laugh while shaking their head. They may even ask questions to gain understanding. It becomes clear that there is not only discomfort, but they are actively making a decision that will inform whether or not they will buy into your request.

When an employee is in a reluctant state, your next move is critical. If you push at all, you will cause resistance. Instead, you must provide for their immediate needs. Invite your employees alongside you so they can slowly, incrementally build buy-in for the change. Then you can confidently embark on the change journey together. The key is for your employees to voluntarily stand beside you so you all can move forward with change together. What takes time during this process is guiding them through reluctance using curiosity, transparency, and patience.

Develop curiosity. Instill a level of curiosity within your employee so they show interest in the change. This can be accomplished through simple questions about their role and how they would like to improve their workflows.

Offer transparency. Your employee most likely does not have knowledge of the change yet, or the knowledge they have is incomplete as it was most likely hearsay through others. Invite them into the dialogue and discuss ways a change can benefit them. Also share how you plan to navigate the change yourself.

Remain patient. Everyone will move at their own pace and sometimes they may wait to see how long you will wait for them. This may not be an act of defiance or that they are trying to "test" you, it could simply be that they are building up the courage to trust you.

Are you ready to take this a step further? Imagine what would happen if your employee was standing six feet to your left and you proceeded to walk toward them, placed your hand on their shoulder, and said, "Hey, we are launching new software that you will need to begin using in a few weeks." You'll probably be met with immediate skepticism or reluctance because you are bringing this new information to their space, with limited clarity, and quite literally transferring unexpected responsibility onto them.

If you continue to push change onto your employee by pressing more firmly against their shoulder, you are creating pressure and tension between you. Let's say you continue by explaining, "You will need to document all your current processes and transfer all your data to the new system so we can officially launch by the end of the month." With growing pressure, your employee will enter a flight-or-fight mode that will push them into a state of resistance. As soon as we feel cornered, we will either push back or find an escape route. When your employee is in a state of resistance, you will not be able to move forward through change. Their energy and focus is zeroed in on what they are currently experiencing, and cannot be refocused until you bring them back to a balanced state of mind.

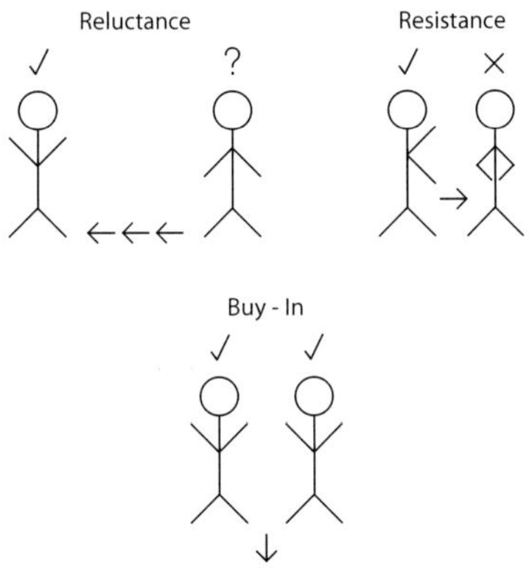

When we push change on someone, resistance is inevitable. This will impede your goal to move forward. Unless you are willing to take the time to bring each employee alongside you and move forward together, then you will fight an uphill battle and perhaps never reach a true state of change adoption. Keeping your employees in a balanced state and providing for their needs when they may be reluctant will prevent them from reaching resistance.

Respond to Resistance

Think of a software system that you are currently using. What are some concerns, complaints, or hesitations you have about that software? Go ahead, list at least five below:

1. ______________________________

2. ______________________________

3. ______________________________

4. ______________________________

5. ______________________________

These are all valid thoughts and I'm sure they could lead to feelings of annoyance, frustration, and maybe even anger at times. I know there isn't a quick fix, but maybe there are some things that can be done to alleviate those feelings.

How did it feel to create that list? How did you feel reading the paragraph after the list? Simply having the opportunity to vocalize concerns and frustrations is freeing.

When working in higher education, I transitioned to a university that already implemented a software platform for student clubs and organizations. After sending an email to all the users and receiving a bounce back rate of eighty-eight percent, I quickly realized that although the software was considered "implemented," adoption by the students was extremely limited given the number of invalid or outdated email addresses in the system. It was time for a relaunch and yours truly was positioned to take on the challenge. All the student organization leaders were invited to an in-person workshop and 152 students attended. I had a hunch that the lack of engagement in the software was a result of how it was initially introduced to the students. Therefore, the workshop began by giving students a single prompt: "All right students, I want to hear all your concerns or frustrations with the software. Let 'er rip!" They were encouraged to shout out all the negative thoughts they had regarding the software. I was not entirely prepared for the influx of responses; some students were even standing on chairs making sure their voices were heard. My goal was to give them a safe space to share and ensure that every single concern was acknowledged and affirmed. My responses included statements such as, "That's a great point, thank you for bringing that up," or "Oh, that's interesting, I'm curious to know more." This continued for about fifteen minutes. It was evident that the students needed me to listen to all their negative feelings and validate their experiences. After all, what they were saying was not a personal attack on me, we were simply trying to solve a problem. Once feeling heard, they trusted me to redirect the discussion toward discovering solutions.

The students were then asked to share all the top challenges they were facing while managing student organizations. Two volunteers were behind me writing all the thoughts on a whiteboard. Some of the challenges included managing membership, collecting dues, staying on top of their budgets, or recruitment. I followed this by asking them to give me fifteen minutes to solve all the problems they listed. Several students laughed and others said, "There is no way, you can't do it." A few even said, "Let's see you try!" At this point I knew their curiosity was swarming. Alas, I began walking the students through a live demo of the software. My volunteer crossed off all thirty-seven challenges as I demonstrated how the software solved each problem the students were facing. The workshop resulted in expanded adoption and consistent use by seventy-nine percent of registered users.

Nothing I did during this workshop was magic. I simply chose to give the students space to share, listen to their concerns, and affirm their feelings. I gave them the capacity to hear a solution. If I didn't yield the floor and listen to them first, they would not have had the capacity to listen to me. What if you gave your employees the opportunity to share thoughts and concerns in a safe environment? Think about concerns, complaints, and hesitations you have heard from your team about other software systems. When they expressed these thoughts, how did you respond?

An affirming response isn't: "But the software will help us with..." or "But it's going to benefit you... so don't worry about that," or "Actually the vision is..." An affirming response truly validates their thoughts and feelings such as: "Yes, you're right. The software doesn't have that feature yet and I think that could be a great feature request." Or, "Yes, you're right. There are more details that we have to add to the system. I am really curious to know what information is bogging you down." Not responding with a rebuttal is going to help your employees feel like they are heard and will give them a sense of freedom. Now you can invite them to be a part of the solution. They will begin to think, "Finally, you've heard me. How can we work together to get through this?" It is important to give your employees the opportunity to vent and your role is to listen and affirm.

Give your employees the microphone first. Keep yourself quiet. Listen and affirm their feelings. Once they feel heard, they'll have the capacity to listen to you. New software should be a solution to solve real-life problems that your employees are facing day after day. If you are not giving them space to share and validating their hesitations and concerns first, then you are not doing your job as a leader.

Determine the Cause

How do we determine the cause of employee resistance? Simply listen. As we've discussed, feeling heard is powerful because it frees up space for an open mind. Try to empathize with and respect your employee's resistance. Although we will never fully understand their perspective, we can do our best to try and it will not go unnoticed. All change is accompanied by some type of reluctance, and you must be willing to work with it rather than argue it away. It is essential that you let personal pride and emotions sit on the sidelines because the focus is not about you anymore and it is not about your organization. Your focus needs to be on your employees, their experiences, and what they are going through. How can you achieve this? By giving your time and energy, asking about their experiences, and using a basic listening sequence. Ivey, Packard, and

Ivey (2019) provide four basic listening skills that serve as a helpful guide:

1. **The proper use of open and closed questions**—use open-ended questions to allow the employee to respond freely and limit closed-ended questions that would usually elicit specific information.

2. **The application of observation skills**—recognize and appreciate all verbal and nonverbal cues as they offer insight into your employee's experience.

3. **Encouraging, paraphrasing, and summarizing what was said**—use verbal and nonverbal cues to show that you are listening. Provide an overview or summary of what you believe you heard.

4. **Reflection and validation of feelings**—state the essential feelings that have been communicated to you.

Step Back and Evaluate

As you are exploring the root of your employee's reluctance, considering factors that may influence their perspective can offer further guidance in how to respond. Assess the person's current state of mind, workload, connection with the rest of the team, and how they have interacted with the software thus far. This type of evaluation requires time for reflection, so try not to rush through it! Ask yourself a series of questions that provide additional awareness into your employee's perspective, such as:

- **How familiar is this person with the new software?**

  If they have no familiarity, then start with the steps to create curiosity and prompt exploration. Understand what their current challenges are and share how the new tool could be a solution.

- **What are their frustration or stress levels at the moment?**

  Try not to present new software to your employees when they are feeling stressed. If they are already feeling overwhelmed, the introduction of something new will feel like added work instead of a helpful tool. If possible, wait until your employees are in a good state of mind. Consider how their workload fluctuates each day of the week and at various times of day and then plan accordingly. Perhaps even help take something off their plate or grab a bite to eat together and then talk about it.

- **What level of impact does this employee have on the future success of the new software in this organization?**

  If your employee will be absolutely critical to the success of the software, then they deserve more of your time and attention to ensure they are fully prepared for the transition and bought into the vision. Early involvement and transparency is paramount.

- **What influence do they have among other users?**

  Identify whether this employee is heavily influential to others in your company. If so, their opinion matters more than you might think. Spend more time with them and bring them into the conversations early so you can leverage this influence in a positive way to help other employees through the change process.

- **What approach might this person respond to best?**

  Each employee has different needs when presented with change. Some will respond best by doing their own research online, others will need to process it out loud, and some will benefit from discussing the change with their co worker rather than discussing it with you. Either way, encourage a route that is best suited for them.

- **Is there a single part of the new software that they don't connect with?**

  Sometimes people become extremely concerned about a single, seemingly minor quirk of a new software system. However, if we can work through this one hang-up, they will most likely be on board with everything else. Try your best to reduce or remove any of these obstacles that stand in the way of adoption. If it is something that can't be overcome, work alongside your employee to find a quality solution. Explore options such as submitting a feature request, using a third-party integration, or creating a quality workaround. Although an ideal solution to their concern may not be available at the time, discuss a plan to move forward while ensuring the rest of the software adds overall value to this employee's role. Essentially, make sure use of the new tool is undeniably "worth it" for the employee.

Use any additional insight gained through the evaluation to create a sort of "resistance profile" about your employee. Compile information they have shared with you directly, concerns their peers may have enlightened you to, and perspective from this reflection. Together, this knowledge will add clarity to understanding your employee's resistance and prepare you for adequately responding to their needs.

Navigate Your Response

Now that you have heard your employee's thoughts and evaluated their perspective, you can determine how you will respond to them. Not to add pressure here, but how you navigate your response is crucial and will either make or break your employee's willingness to adopt the new software. Let's get in the right headspace first...take a deep breath, humble yourself by putting your own agendas aside, and focus on the needs of your employee. Throughout your response, be sure to remain on the same team as your employee, the goal is to find a solution together. Just remember, you need your employee to voluntarily stand beside you, so create a space where you can safely move forward together.

Provide reassurance to alleviate stress. Explain that they are not alone, and that you will be by their side every step of the way to ensure their needs are met throughout the change process.

Communicate the "why" and how the change benefits them. Focus on your employee by discussing how the new software will positively benefit them in their role. At this moment, they may not be concerned about the big picture of the company as much.

Involve them in the change process. Ask your employee their opinions regarding the implementation and rollout. If the conversation is relatively positive, express how valuable they are to the team and ask if they would like a higher level of involvement in the software implementation.

Provide adequate training and support. Ask what specific resources they need to be successful. Make sure that they have the right support for their role and show them where to find help when needed.

Recognize and reward them for their efforts. Communicate your appreciation for their past contributions to the organization and even their willingness to have a conversation with you regarding the new software.

Be patient and persistent. Provide space for your employee to share and be heard, while communicating that the change will be taking place. As a valued employee, you would love for them to be on board.

As you work through your response, keep in mind a few dos and don'ts that could disrupt your progress:

- Don't "sell" the new tool to your users. Rather find their challenge and make the software the solution.
- Don't tell them all the cool tools the software has. Instead, select a few tools that may directly benefit their work.
- Don't use a rehearsed "pitch." Help your employee feel important, like an "insider" by catering your response to their specific needs.
- Don't overpromise. Be confident that you can deliver on every word and follow through.
- Don't share something that isn't true. Get your facts straight early on and then remain honest, authentic, and transparent when discussing the change.
- Don't stand behind something you don't believe in. Ensure you remain passionate about the change yourself.

Authenticity is key; your employees know you well enough to see the truth if you are disingenuous. So remain authentic throughout the entire process as this is your greatest chance to build trust. If you are struggling to gain ground, leverage the employee's peers to discover the source of the hesitation. Influencers in your organization can be your allies as well, so secure their buy-in and let them do the talking.

Build Resilience

By listening to your employees and intentionally responding to their needs, they will begin to develop change resilience. Resilience is having the capacity to recover and persevere when met with obstacles. Whether the obstacle is a minor bump in the road or knocks them off their feet, resilience is measured by a person's ability to bounce back and not allow the obstacle to completely derail them. Your employees have five critical needs in order to build change resilience:

1. A sense of purpose and stability
2. Clarity and transparency
3. Space to process emotions
4. Support and resources
5. Balanced leadership and guidance

We will know when our employees have developed resilience during change when they encounter a new idea and respond with indifference or curiosity rather than skepticism and reluctance. Their ability to adapt in these moments will carry them through the emotional rollercoaster that follows change, ultimately lessening the burden on you to support them through this. When our employees garner the capacity to navigate their reactions to change, your entire organization becomes more agile and can more easily respond to the ever-changing environment.

8 Commit to the Transition

"Stay committed to your decisions, but stay flexible in your approach."

– Tony Robbins

Now that we have introduced the new software, jump in with both feet and invest yourself fully. Commitment is a choice. It may be tempting to stick to your "old ways" here and there, and this is natural. After all, the path of least resistance will always be appealing. Remind yourself that you intentionally made the change for a purpose that supersedes any small obstacles you will face as a result. I have witnessed several leaders make a change and then second-guess their decision or delay full commitment to the change. You might catch yourself saying, "Let's just use a portion of the new software and introduce the rest in phases," or "We'll just keep this spreadsheet as a backup." Statements such as these not only delay the inevitable, but immediately communicate hesitation to your employees, making you appear unsure of whether you trust the new system. Try not to maintain old practices after transitioning to the new software because you don't feel "ready" yet. Doing so will most likely double the work with little reward; not to mention higher chances of mistakes and more frustration for everyone. You have asked your team to step outside their comfort zone, so you need to model this same courage. Are you willing to put both feet into this puddle with your team? If not, your employees will also have one foot in and one foot out... and that creates skepticism. How are you going to get people on board if you are not committed yourself?

Provide the Continued Support

As part of your transition plan, invest adequate time and support toward training your employees. Keep in mind that a healthy balance of training methods is always important. Some step-by-step training is appropriate through recorded videos and written guides. However, training that is designed to help employees understand concepts, make connections, and practice use cases is much more effective through live in-person or virtual sessions. This gives your employees the chance to ask questions, request repeats, and engage in dialogue. Think about a time when you were trying to learn a challenging concept by watching a video and the dots just weren't connecting. You may have rewatched the video, but still didn't find the clarity you needed. I'm sure you felt some frustration and perhaps looked for another video that explained the concept in a different way. Maybe you even gave up trying to understand it. Well, if your employees are facing this same frustration while watching training videos or reading guides, their interest and commitment in learning the new software is going to waver. Unstable commitment is not something you can afford right now. If that isn't convincing you to invest in live training yet, a bonus to hosting live training is that you can hold your employees accountable for actively participating. They will feel that you are investing in their learning process, while you can feel confident they received the training they needed. It's a win-win.

In addition to training, offer easy access to helpful resources before and after the launch date. The type of resources can vary, giving your employees several options that suit their unique needs. Here are a few simple ideas:

- Create printed and digital "cheat sheets" or quick reference guides that provide step-by-step instructions for accomplishing tasks within the software.
- Introduce your employees to the software company's support services and ensure they know how to access support when needed.
- Show your employees how they can access the help desk or resource knowledge base for the software.
- Assemble and share an internal FAQ list to initial questions you anticipate your employees might ask.
- Ask your employees to outline or list the steps they will take to complete various tasks using the software. Not only will this exercise give them clarity, but the step-by-step guides will serve as references for them in the future.
- Connect your employees to the greater community of others who use the same software. Online community forums, chats, or social media groups are

often formed by users to discuss best practices, share tips and tricks, and ask questions. Encouraging employees to join these communities will help them feel a greater sense of connection and give them immediate access to practical resources.

When putting together resources, ask yourself, "What factors or obstacles could prevent my employees from committing to this transition?" Your answers will serve as a guide for ways to proactively set your team up for success. The time spent creating resources now will save you time in the future as you can use them when onboarding and training all new employees as well.

Set a Launch Date

Once you've implemented the software, conduct all your business through it. Don't give yourself or your employees another option. Make clear that you are fully transitioning on a specific date and all related business will be conducted through the software with no exceptions. Of course, give your employees plenty of time to prepare and ensure they are properly equipped prior to the launch date.

Organizations that fail to follow through with a hard launch or "cutover" date often linger in "old" systems because that is where their historic data is stored. In preparation for the launch date, add all essential and historical information to the new system and limit access to this information elsewhere. Turning the new software into a "data repository" adds value to the system. Your employees will begin leaning on it as their source of information and its use becomes part of their routine. Explore your options for how to best accomplish the data transfer by leveraging built-in or assisted importing provided by the software company. If you would like to maintain backup data files of information that is stored in the new system, save them in a protected place where your employees do not have immediate access to them. Your employees will always fall back to what they are comfortable using, so if they are used to accessing information from spreadsheets, they may hunt down the backup files before accessing the information they need through the new software. You have done all the legwork up front to navigate the change process with your employees, now is the time when you hold your ground in a calm and assertive manner.

Reinforce the Change

Remember that the value provided by software is only as good as the information supplied by your employees. In puts that are inconsistent, incomplete, or simply nonexistent will jeopardize its value. If you are not staying on top of how the software is used, then the data in your software becomes unreliable. A hard cutover date is much easier in theory than actually putting it into practice because software adoption is ongoing and will truly never end. Therefore, we must reinforce the change until it sticks. You will find the need to redirect and remind your employees to continue using the system.

Let's say that all your business communications are to be conducted through the new system, yet some employees still choose to send you communication via text messages.

How you respond here is critical and sets the stage for all future software adoption. You have a few options:

1. Respond to the text message with business as usual. Sometimes it feels easier than fighting an uphill battle.
2. Reply to the text message and then kindly remind them to communicate through the new software in the future.
3. Not respond to their text message and only reply to communications that are sent through the new software.

Choosing the first option will result in a failed adoption. By allowing your employees to continue operating in the same manner as before the change, you are giving them permission to ignore the new process and are ultimately reinforcing their former, ineffective behaviors. The second option is okay during the first few weeks you are using the new software. Your employees may genuinely forget or slip back into their former habits, so a reminder never hurts! However, do not drag this out and be sure to put your foot down after a set number of reminders. The third option is always the most difficult, but the most necessary. If you feel uncomfortable with simply not responding, then share with your team that after a specified date you will not be responding to their communications unless they are sent through the software. Also, emphasize the value of the change by sharing the value of using the new system to communicate. After that date, be persistent and unwavering. While this may feel harsh, you are actually providing your employees with structure that they can count on and clarity that reduces uncertainty.

Continue Training

Train as you go. Rather than overwhelming employees by training on the entire software at once, set up small training sessions and discussions for continued conversations so they can absorb the information in smaller doses and catch on slowly. Some training can be saved for after the launch. Post-launch training will also help the new software stay top-of-mind more often—rather than being set on the back burner. Begin by listing all the necessary training topics that need to be covered for each employee role. Then prioritize them in order of urgency and importance. What are the minimum essential training topics that must be covered for each employee to do their job effectively? These are the topics that must be covered before launching the new software. All other training topics are a bonus and can be covered after the launch date to help your employees optimize their use of the tool. Offering ongoing training not only keeps your employees engaged throughout the months after the launch, but also communicates your commitment to its success.

Share "did you knows" or tips and tricks with your employees periodically to extend their enthusiasm about the new software and encourage them to explore more possibilities with its features. Several software companies have newsletters or mailing lists that you can join to receive updates and use case ideas. Online communities and forums are also a great source for tool tips. If you don't have time to drive continued discovery, delegate this job to an employee who has demonstrated excitement about the new solution.

Many software companies host in-person or virtual events such as webinars, workshops, and user conferences that provide opportunities for expanded learning and networking. Attendance at these events can elevate your employees' engagement and interest in the tool. In fact, many of these events are designed to do the heavy lifting for you by providing training and support, while instilling a sense of connection to the software and the company that supports it. Taking advantage of user events, especially those that are in-person, could help your employees develop an affinity toward the new system, resulting in greater enthusiasm for its use and success. Not to mention, investment toward their participation in such events will help your employees feel like valued key players.

Offer Incentives

Remember, old habits die hard, so create incentives for the change. Your role at this time is to provide motivational incentive to follow through and ensure the new software is embedded into everyday practice. Begin by asking yourself, "How have my employees been motivated to carry an idea forward in the past?" Could any of those motivators be used as an incentive to drive adoption for this software?

Establish milestones and celebrate the progress. Share successes that occur as a result of the change (no matter how small) to keep key players engaged. Milestones can be as simple as employees logging their hours in the system for a number of consecutive days, processing a certain number of invoices through the new software, or increasing the percentage of leads that are converted to customers. Refer back to the outcomes and goals you originally set out to accomplish to determine which milestones will be most valuable for your organization. Also, be sure to plan team celebrations for reaching each milestone. When you celebrate as a team, everyone will feel as though they had a hand in the transition, which reinforces the need for continued buy-in and commitment. The type or extent of the celebration is up to your discretion as you know your team best.

Recognize employees who are dedicated to the change. Those who are consistently using the new software add stability to the transition and quickly become models for others. Make sure they know that you notice their efforts. Gather direct feedback from them, have them share their experiences during staff meetings, and ask them to inform you of the tweaks and updates that need to be made to the new system. Consider giving these employees company swag or see if the software company has any swag items that can be given or purchased to reward your employees when they are demonstrating commitment to using the new tool.

Reward those who take risks with the new software. Be on the lookout for employees who take it upon themselves to train their peers, create helpful resources, conduct research, or discover unique ways to use the solution. These are your champions. They may quickly become "power users" and other employees may begin perceiving them as the "go-to" people for any questions about the new software. Employees in this position are often "rewarded" with extra work and responsibilities which could quickly lead to burnout and diminish their eagerness to go above and beyond. Their dedication to the transition deserves meaningful recognition and reward. At minimum, write acknowledgment notes and thank them for being pioneers in the new processes. Take it a step further by giving them special rewards, sending them to professional development events, or providing extra benefits such as time off or a financial bonus.

Add Value to the Software

Add as much value to the new solution as possible so your employees choose to use it. People naturally use tools that provide added benefit, so the more you can pack the new software full of value, the more your employees will be driven to put it to use. When encouraging college students to increase their use of a new tool, I had to make it worthwhile for them. This software needed to become their "go-to" resource any time they had a question, sought out information, or even wanted to get something done. My goal was to position it as the first thing that came to mind when they were managing their student organization. To accomplish this, we filled the software with everything they could possibly need, want, or perhaps didn't even realize was available to them. Adding resources was helpful, but we couldn't stop there. We had to make the software desirable. Here are some ideas to get you started:

- Save quick references in the software that provide information they need on a frequent basis in a simple, easy-to-access manner. This can be information that is directly related to the software itself or information that is relevant to other business processes. Ask yourself, "What directories, spreadsheets, or even sticky note reminders do my employees usually have on-hand for quick reference?" Store information such as employee manuals, account numbers, contact directories, inventory lists, and more.

- Enable tools within the software that make your employees' lives easier. Maybe there is a way to save them steps in their day-to-day processes, or perhaps there are some automatic real-time reports that can be used to save time crunching numbers and building manual reports. Think about each employee's responsibilities and determine how you can ease their everyday burdens. This will position the software as a tool that "solves their problems" and it will pay off!

- Make the software a part of your team culture by adding an element of fun. Think of all the tools it offers and brainstorm ways that you can use them to bring excitement and fun engagement to your culture. Perhaps include a quote of the week on the communication feed, build out team quizzes or host a sports fantasy draft with the form builder, add employee birthdays to the calendar, have each employee upload a family photo in the files, create a team recipe book in the documents, or even ask each employee to update their profile with a new joke each week. Any layer of fun you can add to the system will encourage your employees to keep coming back to the new software, simply out of curiosity if nothing else!

- Situate the new software as a conduit for all other tools. Whether you build out integrations with other systems, enable single sign-on to easily access them, or you simply include links that help you navigate to them; providing access to other tools through your new software adds immediate value. By making it a hub or one-stop-shop to access all other tools and resources, you are centralizing the new solution and encouraging employees to depend on it.

- Seek ways that you can continue streamlining processes by connecting the software to other platforms and systems that employees use on a daily basis. Communicate the role that each tool plays in your organization, so employees understand the purpose for each and the relationship between them.

A key principle to remember is the higher the value, the higher the use. Give your employees a reason to use the new software on a daily basis in addition to their standard responsibilities. Turn it into something that your employees won't want to live without!

Follow Through on Promises

When we first set out to introduce new software in our organization, we had big plans in mind. Some of those plans may have shifted a bit since then, though we were sure to specify our goals while building a case for the change process. The priorities, goals, and outcomes agreed upon by your team before the software launch should remain front and center even after the launch. This is a great time to revisit the promises you made to your team and gauge how well you are following through on them. I caution you to not solely rely on your own perceptions, but rather ask your employees how they feel the transition is going. Users often develop concerns about a new solution after they start using it for a while. Either the software is falling short of expectations, users are discovering limitations that impact their workflow, or it might be more cumbersome to use than they originally thought. Plan ahead for concerns that will arise by scheduling group check-in meetings with your employees throughout the implementation and post-implementation to see how they are handling the transition. Doing so will give your employees time and space to share their thoughts and will further increase trust and followership. These discussions may also illuminate areas where you can step in, problem solve, and overcome barriers before they become larger issues that negatively impact your organizational success.

9 Reap the Benefits of Change

"Companies that change may survive, but companies that transform thrive. Change brings incremental or small-scale adaptations, while transformation brings great improvements that ripple through the future of an organization."

\- Nick Candito

The whole point of going through this process is to implement new software that adds value to your organization by streamlining processes, increasing efficiencies, or improving effectiveness. You will only know if you have accomplished this by assessing your progress toward reaching your goals and outcomes. Refer back to chapter five where we planned our assessment measures for the intended outcomes of the new software. This plan now serves as a roadmap to evaluate your success. Schedule consistent audits to review whether you are trending toward and accomplishing your goals. It is recommended to audit at minimum twice each year, but quarterly is ideal as you can catch issues early on and have more flexibility to course-correct if needed. Enjoy every moment of achieving the goals you set out for with the new software and recognize its impact on the greater organization!

Beyond the software adoption itself, keeping your employee experience front and center while navigating this change process presents several additional benefits that can serve as "bonuses." First, you are laying the foundation for an agile organization culture that will carry forward well beyond this implementation. This sets your team up for success by preparing them for future change that is essential to sustainable organizational growth. Having successfully navigated change and experiencing the light at the end of the tunnel gives your employees confidence that they can make it through future change. You'll probably even notice them approach change with optimism rather than skepticism. Fostering a culture that is change-resilient reduces resistance when your employees approach new initiatives.

Second, by focusing on your employees' experiences, you are building insurmountable trust with them. If they feel heard and supported throughout the change process, they will also feel an increased sense of value in the company. Establishing a trusting leader-follower relationship is always worth the time and investment because it breeds loyalty among your employees. Reflecting back upon all my previous supervisors, one stands out among the rest. This supervisor never hesitated to invest time, energy, and even funding toward building a relationship with me. We had frequent one-on-one meetings where they checked in on my personal and professional experiences. They intentionally sought out my perspective when making organizational decisions. They listened as I shared life challenges and even connected by sharing their own challenges. I never once felt like an inconvenience or an interruption to their work. Feeling valued in this way built unwavering trust and you better believe I followed their lead through thick and thin because of the strength of our relationship.

To this day, I still reach out to them as a mentor and a friend. The time you invest in your employees now will be paid in dividends later, when you need them to have your back.

Third, you are engaging your employees in a forward-thinking process that will prompt them to continue thinking ahead, keeping your organization on the cusp of growth opportunities. Before you know it, your employees may begin presenting new initiatives to you! This is when you know you have instilled lasting change. You are modeling strategic thinking, commitment to priorities, effective execution, and above all, a people-first approach to change. Employees will learn from your leadership and emulate your approach so you are truly equipping them with the tools they need to initiate change themselves. By offering transparency and opportunities for involvement throughout the transition, you are giving your employees an enriching and empowering professional development experience. Higher engagement also means higher commitment to your organization and ultimately less employee turnover. All parties benefit.

Lastly, employees who work together to navigate challenges and accomplish a common goal often form closer bonds with one another. Simply put, leading change with mindfulness, transparency, and sound strategy could actually become a team builder that strengthens relationships among your employees. I'll never forget the bond that grew between myself and a coworker when we were both tasked to implement, train, and onboard a new software system across our organization. I had recently started and managed a completely different part of the department than my coworker. In fact, the two of us were opposites in every way. We approached our work from opposing perspectives, we were motivated by very different means, and our priorities couldn't have been further apart. However, the one commonality that our supervisor saw in us was our excitement for strategy-building and process development. Now, I'm not entirely sure whether our supervisor intended for us to become closer as a result of working on this project together, but my coworker and I became best friends in the process. We were so excited about the project that we voluntarily spent nights and weekends in coffee shops, libraries, and each other's homes working on the software implementation. Not to mention the in-depth discussions that took place over the occasional glass of wine. Although I no longer work alongside her, she was and will remain my best friend and confidant even though we still have completely opposite personalities, perspectives, and lifestyles. I hope the connection that grew between the two of us, as a result of implementing new software, inspires you to look deeper than the implementation itself and zero in on the people behind the software as you lead the charge. After all, technology comes and goes, but the people behind the scenes are the true strength of your organization.

Acknowledgments

The collaborative nature of writing a book is undeniable and I attribute much of this accomplishment to those who eagerly embarked on this authorship journey with me.

> To my family who provided endless
> strength, stability, and courage.
>
> To my former employees and clients
> who taught me how to be a leader.
>
> To my close friends who kept my thoughts
> spinning and jumped at any opportunity
> to help.
>
> Namely, Tyler Widdick, Mai Nguyen,
> Ashley Strom, and Jess Tate.

Thank you for volunteering your time to support my growth.

About the Author

During her time working in higher education and with various industry start-ups, **Dr. Anna Hunter** discovered a great passion for helping organizations maximize employee engagement while guiding them toward sustainable success. She is motivated by the change process and aims to instill change resilience by leading people through resistance. Dr. Anna earned a Doctorate of Education in Organizational Leadership, with an emphasis in transformation and change. She also holds a Master of Science in Counseling and College Student Development. Dr. Anna is a certified Change Management Specialist, Gallup Certified Strengths Coach, certified MBTI Practitioner, and trained Talking Circle Keeper for conflict reconciliation.

Dr. Anna is a coach, trainer, and group facilitator who helps individuals and organizations develop the skills necessary for achieving growth and self-sustaining success. Areas of expertise include adult learning, employee engagement, organizational change management, software adoption and management, and transformational leadership. She also specializes in process improvement, group conflict reconciliation, program and event management, marketing and influence, leadership development, meeting facilitation, learning outcome development, and assessment integration.

Dr. Anna would love to speak with you! Contact her by visiting **www.anna-hunter.com**.

References

BetterCloud. 2023. *State of SaaSOps.* https://www.bettercloud.com/resources/stateofsaasops23/

Fisher, John. 2012. *The Process of Transition.* https://www.businessballs.com/change-management/personal-change-stages-john-fisher/

Fullen, Michael. 2001. *Leading in a Culture of Change.* San Francisco, CA: Jossey-Bass.

Grundy, Tony. 1993. *Implementing Strategic Change.* London, UK: Kogan.

Ivey, Allen E., Packard, Norma Gluckstern, Ivey, Mary Bradford. 2019. *Basic Attending Skills, Foundations of Empathic Relationships and Problem Solving.* 6th Edition. San Diego, CA: Cognella Academic Publishing.

Rogers, Everett M. 1962. *Diffusion of Innovations.* New York, NY: Free Press.

Schlossberg, Nancy K. 2008. *Overwhelmed: Coping with Life's Ups and Downs.* 2nd Edition. Lanham, MD: M. Evans.